THE EDGAR CAYCE READER

This unique, comprehensive volume is a remarkable demonstration of the wide range of Edgar Cayce's life's work.

For the first time in one book, Edgar Cayce's insights are offered on a number of consistently fascinating topics: Karma, psychoanalysis, automatic writing, telepathy, out-of-body travel, reincarnation, to name just a few.

The interpretation of Edgar Cayce's thoughts on these topics are absolutely authentic, having been written by writers who have long studied the Cayce Readings and who have been approved by the Edgar Cayce Association for Research and Enlightenment in Virginia Beach, Va.

For the many hundreds of thousands of people who have become intrigued with, and who have benefited from, Edgar Cayce, this book will be a basic, invaluable addition to their Cayce reference library.

THE EDGAR CAYCE READER

The almost fifteen thousand telepathic-clairvoyant readings of the late Edgar Cayce include material on an exceptionally wide variety of subjects. While in general it falls into the categories of mental, physical, and spiritual, the research breaks down into studies in the fields of psychology, parapsychology, philosophy, religion, history, pre-history, and medicine. *The A.R.E. Journal,* the quarterly publication of the Association for Research and Enlightenment, brings to its readers articles based on careful research into the Cayce records, as well as studies which correlate with those data. *THE EDGAR CAYCE READER* presents some of the articles previously published in the *Journal* as a sampling of the research being done and as an illustration of the broad scope of the information in these records.

THE EDGAR CAYCE READER

under the editorship of
HUGH LYNN CAYCE

PAPERBACK LIBRARY

New York

CONTENTS

INTRODUCTION

WHO WAS EDGAR CAYCE?

The ten books which have been written about him have totaled more than a million in sales, and more than ten other books have devoted sections to his life and talents. He has been featured in dozens of magazines and hundreds of newspaper articles dating from 1900 to the present. What was so unique about him?

It depends on whose eyes you look at him through. A goodly number of his contemporaries knew the "waking" Edgar Cayce as a gifted professional photographer. Others (predominantly children) admired him as a warm and friendly Sunday School teacher. His own family knew him as a wonderful husband and father.

The "sleeping" Edgar Cayce was an entirely different figure; a psychic known to thousands of people, in all walks of life, who had cause to be grateful for his help; indeed, many of them believe that he alone had either saved or changed their lives when all seemed lost. The "sleeping" Edgar Cayce was a medical diagnostician, a prophet, and a devoted proponent of Bible lore.

In June, 1954, the University of Chicago held him in sufficient respect to accept a Ph.D. thesis based on a study of his life and work: in this thesis the graduate referred to him as a "religious seer." In June of that same year, the children's comic book *House of Mystery* bestowed on him the impressive title of "America's Most Mysterious Man!"

Even as a child on a farm near Hopkinsville, Kentucky, where he was born on March 18, 1877, Edgar Cayce displayed powers of perception which seemed to extend beyond the normal range of the five senses. At the age of six or seven he told his parents that he was able to see and talk to "visions," sometimes of relatives who had recently died. His parents attributed this to the overactive imagination of a lonely child who had been influenced by the dramatic language of the revival meetings which were popular in that section of the country. Later, by sleeping with his head on his schoolbooks, he developed some form of photographic memory which helped him advance rapidly in the country school. This faded, however, and Edgar was only able to complete his seventh grade before he had to seek his own place in the world.

By twenty-one he had become the salesman for a wholesale stationery company. At this time he developed a gradual paralysis of the throat muscles, which threatened the loss of his voice. When doctors were unable to find a physical cause for these conditions, hypnosis was tried, but failed to have any permanent effect.

As a last resort, Edgar asked a friend to help him enter the same kind of hypnotic sleep that had enabled him to memorize his schoolbooks as a child. His friend gave him the necessary suggestions, and once he was in self-induced trance, Edgar came to grips with his own problem. He recommended medication and manipulative therapy which successfully restored his voice and repaired his system.

A group of physicians from Hopkinsville and Bowling Green, Kentucky, took advantage of his unique talent to diagnose their own patients. They soon discovered that Cayce only needed to be given the name and address of the patient, wherever he was, and was then able to "tune in" telepathically on that individual's mind and body as easily as if they were both in the same room. He needed, and was given, no other information regarding any patient.

One of the young M.D.'s, Dr. Wesley Ketchum, submitted a report on this unorthodox procedure to a clinical research society in Boston. On October 9, 1910, *The New York Times* carried two pages of headlines and pictures. From that day on, invalids from all over the country sought help from the "wonder man."

When Edgar Cayce died on January 3, 1945, in Virginia Beach, Virginia, he left well over fourteen thousand documented stenographic records of the telepathic-clairvoyant statements he had given for more than eight thousand different people over a period of forty-three years. These typewritten documents are referred to as "readings."

8

These readings constitute one of the largest and most impressive records of psychic perception ever to emanate from a single individual. Together with their relevant records, correspondence and reports, they have been cross-indexed under thousands of subject-headings and placed at the disposal of psychologists, students, writers and investigators who come in increasing numbers to examine them.

A foundation known as the A.R.E. (The Association for Research and Enlightenment, Inc., P. O. Box 595, Virginia Beach, Virginia, 23451) was founded in 1932 to preserve these readings. As an open-membership research society, it continues to index and catalogue the information, initiate investigation and experiments, and promote conferences, seminars and lectures. Until now its published findings have been made available to its members through its own publishing facilities.

Now Paperback Library has made it possible to present a series of popular volumes dealing with those subjects from the Edgar Cayce readings most likely to appeal to public interest.

This volume brings you a selection of articles previously published in *The A.R.E. Journal,* the quarterly magazine of the Association for Research and Enlightenment. This publication was established in January of 1966 as one of the services for Association membership, now numbering many thousands who are scattered all over the world. Because the records left by the late Edgar Cayce include material on an exceptionally wide variety of subjects, *The Edgar Cayce Reader* includes studies which reflect careful research by psychologists, general medical practitioners, psychiatrists, teachers and interested laymen. These articles as well as the verbatim extracts from the readings not only illustrate the broad scope of information that came through Cayce, but suggest that the data from the readings are continuing to be of practical help in man's search for meaning in his relationship to both his Creator and his fellow man.

—Hugh Lynn Cayce

HOW TO DEVELOP YOUR PSYCHIC ABILITY

Edgar Cayce

Unfortunately, we have all come to think of "psychic" as something very unusual, especially since the dictionary gives as one definition of psychic as follows: "having abnormal powers, especially the power of automatic writing or of conversing in a trance."

If we understood the real meaning of psychic forces, however, we would have a different conception as to the significance of developing such powers within ourselves. Whether we wish to acknowledge it or not, all of us have psychic forces. Whether we want to develop them or not is a different question.

When people go about to develop any special ability or faculty, we know that they go into training with that object in view. One training for the prize ring has certain things that must not be done. In order to develop the ability to use some portion or function of the physical body, specific preparation must be made. One developing the voice trains that special ability or faculty. Certain rules must be followed in order to sing, to play the violin or piano.

What is that faculty which goes through the process of being trained? Is it simply a portion of the physical body?

As we begin to develop such faculties or abilities latent within every individual—such as discernment of color, or the differentiation in how to apply it to visualize or picturize for others something we have seen in nature—these faculties partake of more than just the ability to draw the hand across the palette, the canvas or a piece of paper. Something within is being expressed. What gives the expression? Our psychic forces!

Now let me give you just what "psychic" means and say how it should be properly used. Do not think that every

10

person you hear spoken of as "psychic" has something very peculiar about him; for you are afflicted with the same condition! You are just as peculiar as he; possibly more so.

Webster gives this primary definition of psychic or psychical: "Of or pertaining to the human soul. Of or pertaining to the living principle in man. Sometimes pertaining to the human soul in its relationship to sense, or to appetite, and the outer visible world as distinct from the spiritual for the rational faculties." The second definition is "Of or pertaining to the mind, the mental contrasted within the physical body."

Perception of the physical mind must come through the senses. Development of a faculty within means development of the acuteness of a sense. We know that what we seek to understand or comprehend reaches us physically through the five senses. As we draw comparisons, we get the differentiation and the ability to evaluate tone or color. Just as a photographic print has to go through a certain process in being made, so in perception we develop the power or ability to discern with the faculty we possess.

People are sometimes afflicted with psychic blindness, consisting of an inability to recognize objects as they are seen. I once knew a man who saw everything upside down. He could not see any other way; everything was upside down to him. He was psychically blind!

There are also those who are psychically deaf, which consists of an inability to comprehend the significance of harmony or sounds heard. We have seen people who were able to hear over a telephone but could not hear while sitting in a room talking with anyone; or they could hear while riding on a train but not while walking down the street. That is because some portion of the psychic functioning in the body is deficient.

Then we know from these things that there is a definite faculty within our bodies which we may call psychic forces, or psychic powers. This faculty pertains to the soul and also to something physical. Hence the great difference in the French and in the Grecian definition of psychic. To the French it means "animal" or "carnal"; while the Grecian meaning is "of the soul life." These two meanings are just as foreign to each other as possible! No wonder we

11

find so many different meanings of the word as used by others!

When we use a word, what do we mean to imply or convey to others? This depends upon the ability of those listening—and also upon our ability to describe, through psychic forces, or through the development obtained through psychic forces. Only like begets like; only like can understand like. It is very hard for an engineer to describe to a musician just what his work is like, or for the musician to describe his work to an engineer. This is because of individual training of physical faculties—but also the portion which gives a perfect understanding or comprehension of those physical faculties: that is, the psychic force.

There is also such a thing as psychic medicine, that department of science which treats of mental disease. If the psychic forces are not developed, there's something wrong with the mental abilities, something wrong with the abilities to comprehend. Because the ability to feed our souls (and that is why we are here) depends upon our ability to supply ourselves from our surroundings with that which will enable us to develop the power of comprehension within.

If you are a musician, you can easily understand what is meant by psychic rhythm. It is the rhythmic form in which the mind tends to perceive monotonously repeated stimulation. That's why we pray and why we should also pray audibly, because the sound stimulates the ability to awaken our senses, in order to arouse the forces which will strengthen the psychic abilities within.

Another definition of psychic forces would be found by comparing the finite and infinite. These convey entirely different impressions to our minds.

The finite mind pertains wholly to our faculties or abilities—which may feed the soul, provided we give it whatever may build to sustain its life. But the infinite mind, about which the first question would be, "How can you know the infinite?" cannot be discerned through reason. It is the finite mind which tries to reason, to distinguish and to define by comparison—processes which are only a portion of the faculties called psychic forces. Thus infinite mind is outside the realm of ordinary reasoning. We can comprehend the infinite only by a faculty that is superior to reason. That faculty is the psychic force. One must enter a state in which the finite self no longer exists!

So often we pray as did the old lady who prayed for the hill to be moved; and every morning she looked out and said, "It is still there. I knew it would be."

We haven't gotten out of our finite reasoning self, so that the infinite can come in and aid. We must develop the faculty *between* the finite and the infinite, so that the infinite may become a portion of us. We seek to become one with the infinite by the reduction of our soul to its simplest self—its divine essence—and realize this union and identity.

Now, we might well go back and question how man developed this *personality* (finite) and how he lost his *individuality,* by losing the place he occupied with his Creator, in the beginning. This individuality is ever seeking to find expression through the faculties with which man has been endowed; for through these there may come expressions of the infinite, or God, into our lives.

We know that we have gradually lost our association, by our inability to close off our outer finite selves. In other words, we have thought so much about ourselves and the supplying of the needs of the physical, that we have gratified the fleshly desires until we have forgotten there is still an association of our soul with its Maker. That association is what we may choose to term *psychic forces,* or psychic abilities.

No one would deny that such faculties may be used by those who lose their physical consciousness; or that they may be discerned in a gathering which has been attuned to influences from within or without.

When we attempt to be very close to—or even on speaking terms with—our God, do we expect an answer? When we pray, do we always expect to get an answer? We must lose the finite self and be willing to be used, in whatsoever way or manner He sees fit. "Enoch walked with God, and he was not; for God took him." He was not found among his brethren, because his faith was counted to him for righteousness. If our faith or if our abilities for that psychic faculty we all possess have been so abused and we have allowed them to be ridiculed because we see visions or hear things; then we have built a barrier which

13

prevents the faculties latent within each individual from developing us toward the Infinite.

All that tends to purify and elevate the mind will assist us in this attainment, and will facilitate the approach and re-occurence of these happy conditions. There are, then, different roads by which this end may be reached. The love of beauty which exalts the poet; that devotion to the One; that ascent of present science which makes the ambition of the philosopher; that love and those prayers by which some devout and ardent soul tends in its moral purity towards perfection—these all are the great highways conducting to the heights above the actual and the particular, where we may stand in the immediate presence of the Infinite which shines out from the depths of the soul.

The adherence to the developing of the ability to see and appreciate the beautiful, the pure, and the lovely in everything and everybody we contact—everything within the scope of what affects our body, mind and heart—will develop in us the abilities to be in closer attunement with the Infinite. And this is developing our psychic abilities within.

The answer comes to each one of us, as to whether these abilities are worth developing or not. If we have the proper conception of what psychic means, then we know it is a faculty which exists—has existed, and is ours by birthright; because we are sons and daughters of God. We have the ability to make association with the Spirit; for "God is Spirit and seeks such to worship Him."*

*See John 4:23

June 30, 1932

MENTAL TELEPATHY

Edgar Cayce

Mind reading, or mental telepathy, does exist; we know that. We experience it ourselves every day. Many of us have had the experience of thinking about someone—and that person calls us on the phone. Again, we may have been speaking about certain people, and they walk in the door.

This kind of thing happened to me just a few days ago. We were discussing a subject. As far as I knew, there was no reason on earth for the person involved to come to my home; but as we were speaking of him and his abilities, it happened that he appeared right then.

What caused this? Was it chance—just an everyday occurrence? Or was it that the thought-vibrations between our minds and his mind brought about the conversation?

My experiences have taught me that practically every phase of phenomena may be explained by activities of the subconscious mind. First, let me tell you one of my own experiences along these lines—an experiment I have never repeated! In telling you why not, I can give you my ideas as to how mental telepathy should and should not be used.

While I was operating a photographic studio, a young lady was working in my studio who was really a musician, yet she had become interested in photography and in the phenomena as manifested through me. We had many discussions about the various phases of these phenomena.

One day I said to her that I could force an individual to come to me. She said it was impossible and I told her I would prove it to her. I said this because I had been thinking about the subject and studying it. I felt that I had an inkling of what this great force was—the subconscious mind—which we had been discussing. I believed that one should be able to hold mental images within one's self, by deep concentration; and by seeing another person doing a thing, one could mentally force that person to do it.

The young lady said, "Well, I believe most of the things you've told me, but this is one thing I do not believe. You'll certainly have to show me that."

"All right," I said. "Who are two people you consider it would be impossible for me to influence?"

"You couldn't get my brother to come up here," she said, "and I know you couldn't get Mr. B. to come here, either, because he dislikes you."

I told her that before twelve o'clock the next day her brother would not only come up to the studio, but he would ask me to do something for him. "And the next day before two o'clock," I told her, "Mr. B. will come here."

She shook her head, and said that she couldn't believe anything of the kind.

Now our studio was so arranged that from the second floor we could look into a mirror and see what was going on in the street below. At ten o'clock the next day, I came in and sat down. I sat in meditation about thirty minutes, just thinking about the boy; yet I wondered if perhaps I hadn't overstepped myself in saying he was going to ask me to do something for him, because his sister had told me that he didn't have any patience with the work I did.

After about half an hour of this concentrated thought, I saw the boy pass on the street below, then turn and come up on the steps. He stood there a few seconds, looking up the steps—then walked away. In a few minutes, he turned in again and came up the steps to the second floor.

His sister looked around and said, "What are you doing here?"

The boy sat on the edge of the table, turning his hat around in his hands. Then he said, "Well, I hardly know—but I had some trouble last night at the shop, and you've been talking so much about Mr. Cayce, I just wondered if he couldn't help me out." His sister almost fainted!

The next day, at eleven o'clock, I took my seat in the same chair. The girl said, "I guess you can work it on Mr. B., if you worked it on my brother."

I told her I wouldn't be in when Mr. B. came, because he disliked me so much; and that he wouldn't know why

16

he had come in. She told me afterwards that he did come in about twelve thirty, after I had gone out. She asked him if she could do anything for him. He said, "No, I don't know what I'm doing here—I just came up," and walked out.

Now, to my way of thinking these are examples of mental telepathy, or mind reading—but they show a *forcing of yourself upon someone else*. That's dangerous business! It pertains to the black arts; it's one of those things none of us has a right to do unless we are very sure of what we are doing, and of our motives. Sometimes it might be used well, perhaps at times to control our children in that way. Yet even then it might be dangerous for, as our information says, anyone who would force another to submit to his will is a tyrant! Even God does not force His will upon us. Either we make our will one with His, or we are opposed to Him. Each person has an individual choice.

Then what part may mental telepathy play in our lives—that is the big question. For anything good can also be dangerous. I could mention nothing good but what it also has its misapplication, its mis-use. How then may we use mind reading or mental telepathy constructively?

The best rule I can give is this: Don't ask another person to do something you would not do yourself. The Master never asked such a thing; and let us never ask it.

When the Master went down into Judea, He was asked by one of the noblemen of the district, a Pharisee, to have dinner with him. He accepted immediately. Did He ask who the man was, or why he had asked Him, or why this opportunity was being offered Him? We answer, "No, because He knew these things." Certainly, He knew! So should we, too, know things within our inmost selves. And why should we know things within? We should live right, within our inner selves, so that we know each contact we make is an opportunity to speak according to what we represent, from a spiritual standpoint.

So Jesus accepted this invitation to dinner, and His disciples went with Him. As they sat at the table, a woman of the street came in and washed His feet with tears and wiped them with the hair of her head. She also anointed His feet with precious ointment.

The nobleman thought to himself—as many of us would today—"What kind of man is this? Doesn't he
17

know the kind of person she is?" Jesus, *knowing what was in his mind*, said, "Simon, I have somewhat to say unto thee . . . There was a certain creditor which had two debtors: the one owed five hundred pence, and the other fifty. And when they had nothing to pay, he frankly forgave them both. Tell me therefore, which of them will love him most? Simon answered and said, I suppose that one to whom he forgave the most. And He said unto him, Thou hast rightly judged." (Luke 7:36-50)

Note that Jesus did not say to Simon, "This is what you are thinking about," nor accuse him of being discourteous in that Simon did not provide water for His feet, nor oil to anoint His head. Jesus simply spoke in such a way as to awaken in Simon the realization that he should not find fault with another.

At times, then, we too are able to sense what people are thinking and we may know the trend their thoughts are taking. At such times, our conversation and actions toward them can be such as to *show*—even as the Master showed Simon—that the inmost thoughts can be known to those who are closely associated with the Divine.

We hear a great deal about people acquiring mental powers. The advertisements say, "Be a strong man—control others by your powerful mind." But it's dangerous business trying to control any other person so that he will do *your bidding*. To influence someone mentally, just as we would in his presence, so that he *does God's bidding*, and comes to know light and truth—that's different! Did you ever pray for a person—did you ever get down on your knees and pray to God that someone's life might be changed? That is using mind-power, or telepathy, properly. For the force that changes must be from the Divine Source.

Since that first experience of mine in the studio, I have had others of the same kind. I have tried to demonstrate to people the power of mind; but as I studied these matters more and more, I decided never to do such a thing again. Anyone who wants to control another person, can do it—but beware! The very thing you wish to control in the other person will be the thing that will destroy you—it will become your Frankenstein!

Many of you who have studied something of the history

18

of Atlantis know that such mental forces were highly developed there. Numbers of people were able to think with such concentration that they could bring material things into existence by the very power of their thought. To use such forces for selfish purposes, as they used them, can result only in evil. The greatest sins in the world today are selfishness and the domination of one individual will by another will.

Few people have the desire to, or will allow other individuals to live their own lives. We want to tell them how; we want to force them to live our way and see things as we see them. Most wives want to tell their husbands what they can do; and most husbands want to tell their wives what they can and cannot do. Have you ever stopped to think that no one else answers to God for you? Nor do you answer to God for them.

If a person will seek first to know himself, then the ability to know another's mind will come. Most of those who will practice it for just a little while can develop along this line. But be sure you don't attempt to do God's work! Do your own and you'll have your hands full. It is your business to make your own paths straight—not another's. The straight and narrow path leads directly to Him—by your own manner of living, not by trying to control.

The force of mind exists, just as it did in ancient Atlantis. What happened when the Atlanteans attempted to use that force selfishly? Destruction—for these may be destructive forces. We all have this mental ability; we can all train ourselves to use it to force others to our will. But we have no moral right to do this. We have the right to tell people our own personal experiences and let them decide for themselves; but not to force them, for God calls upon every man, everywhere, to look, to heed, to understand.

When we use the forces within to serve the Creative Forces and God, then we are using them correctly. If they are used for our own selfish interests, they are being abused. Then we become even as the son of perdition—call him whatever we will.

February 15, 1931

19

THE VISIBLE AND THE INVISIBLE

Edgar Cayce

A few weeks ago, I stood up to speak to a Sunday School class, and many more seats were vacant in front of me than were filled. Within myself I felt that I had something to say, and I wondered why so few were present. Then I saw an invisible audience come in and fill practically every seat there—an audience invisible to the others present.

We may rest assured that there is the invisible as well as the visible! We always have with us an invisible audience for our acts—yes, even for every thought. If only we could come to realize this more and more, then we would know His presence abides with us; and if it does not abide with us, it is our own fault or we have blinded ourselves to that which we could have for our very own.

Everyone realizes that we are passing through a period of stress in which we all are expecting something—what, we do not know. Why don't we know what to expect? Why is it impossible to know what is going to happen? Isn't it because we have blinded ourselves to the evidence around us?

We are told by many who have made a study of such matters that we are passing through a certain position in the universe. Astrologers have said that we are reaching that place in space wherein the influences are beginning for the third cycle. Others describe it as a place where we may expect a new race, a new people, a new thought.

Admitting for the moment that this is true: are such influences bearing upon us because we are in such a position in the universe, or are we in such a position because of what we or somebody else has done? It is the same old question arising in our experience day by day when, as the first man asked God, "Am I my brother's keeper?", death was brought into the world. We are still evading the question and blaming someone else for the position we occupy.

We are also told that individuals are being reincarnated into the earth who occupy a position from which they may wield a mighty influence, because of the position they once occupied in the thought of the world. Now they are coming into their own.

Be that as it may; are we not all in the same position as to what we are going to do about it? There is no power that is not ordained of God. Then is it not the plan of the Supreme Force or Power that we call God, that we as individuals are reincarnated into the earth's experience at this time? It has been laid out beforehand.

Then you may say, "Well, you are a fatalist, and believe what's going to happen is going to happen—nothing can change it." No, that isn't answering the question of being our brother's keeper.

We are studying along lines of thought pertaining to development of the inner man, the soul. Within us is that something we call the soul, the entity, the being; and this lives on and on.

We say this is a period of hard times when we all wonder just what is coming to pass, that it is a period when there are to be upheavals. What have we done to prepare ourselves for such happenings? "These things will come about," the Master said, "but the time isn't yet. There shall be wars and rumors of wars. There shall be earthquakes in divers places. There shall be signs in heaven and brother shall rise against brother, nation against nation, but the time isn't yet." (See Matt. 24.)

All these things are coming about. What was the warning beforehand? "If ye fall away, if ye go back and follow after those things pertaining to the desires of your own carnal influences, I will turn my face from you." (See Deut. 31: 16-17).

The invisible face, yes; that which we cannot see, cannot perceive with the five senses. Yet that which may be aroused within us tells us whether or not we are following in the way He would have us go. "My spirit will bear witness with your spirit as to whether ye be the sons of God or not." (See Romans 8: 16)

It doesn't matter how these warnings have come to us. We are now in the midst of the condition, and it is all

21

around us. The changes are coming about. Portions of the earth are going to be wiped away in the next few years; I feel very sure of that. Right away, we want to know if it will happen where we are. What difference does it make, if we are living right?

To be overanxious about ouselves because we are living in the wrong place is to be like the people who came to the old lady living on the frontier. A man came to her and said he wanted to make a place for his family of boys and girls growing up, but he certainly hated to leave all his friends at home. She said, "Well, you'll find it just the same way out here. If you had friends at home, you'll have friends here." The next man who came said that he was glad to get away from the place where he had lived so many years; the people there were all selfish, stingy and hard to get along with. The old lady said, "Brother, you'll find it the same way out here. If you couldn't get along with the folks at home, you won't be able to get along with the folks out here. If you didn't have friends at home, you won't find them here."

So with us. If we are not ready, if we're not making our preparations, it will be only a matter of time before we must pay the penalty—even if we don't happen to be among the first taken away in a moment.

How do we know these changes are going to take place? We don't know, except by the signs that have been told us, and that we are experiencing. For the outward appearances, the things visible around us, are mere shadows of the things that really exist and are coming about. When, as the Master said, we see these changes coming, we know it is because people acted within themselves and toward their neighbor in such a way as to bring about these changes.

The first command was: "Be fruitful, multiply, subdue the earth." (Gen. 1: 28) That means obtain the knowledge of all these things that are here in the earth. And there isn't a thing in the earth that isn't a manifestation of God. Do we show forth our appreciation for the things about us, or do we say "Gimmie, gimmie, gimmie," and try to draw it all into ourselves? Are we our brother's keeper—or is our brother keeping us?

Life isn't a bit different today from what it was a million years ago. Life is One. God is Life—whether in the oyster, the tree, or in us. Life is God and a manifestation of Him. Man can make a beautiful tree, but he can't give it life. He can make a beautiful egg, but he can't give it that which will make it reproduce itself. *What is that something which can reproduce life,* except Life itself, or God? It is the invisible that is within us, and completely around us.

If thoughts are deeds, our constructive and positive thinking will aid in building or establishing that which will bring peace, harmony, joy, love—the fruits of the spirit. What is the Spirit? That which we can comprehend only by the application of it, by what we do for someone else.

We had a very beautiful illustration of this thought in our Sunday School lesson this morning. The Master had spent Himself in giving out to others. He had grown tired and weary, and it was necessary that he rest physically, for he was then a man. Something had been taken out of Him, in order to give constructive influences to offset those destructive influences in the lives of those He had contacted. He was asleep, at sea. The boat began to fill and the disciples became uneasy. They went and woke Him: "Carest thou not that we perish?" He rebuked the wind, and the sea became calm. Let me ask: Did that power *go out* of the Master, or did it *come into* Him? It came into Him—the peace, the calm—because He was of the Creative Forces that would manifest. *In the giving out, it came in.* And as we too give out, to make this a better world for others to live in, peace and harmony and understanding—fruits of the Spirit—come into us.

Shall we go and do wonderful things? Shall we stand on the corner and preach? Of course, if we are called to do such things, then we should do them. Yet perhaps we shall just speak a kind word to our next-door neighbor, to the child we meet in the street, to the lame dog we see—or to anything or anybody that is a manifestation of God. Just speaking the kind word that brings hope to those who are losing hope; speaking the cheery word to those who are discouraged; as we can do these things, we give out that which we have received. "Freely ye have received, freely give." For not all are called to be healers, not all

23

preachers; but each of us can do what our hands find to do, magnifying the Spirit and the fruits of the Spirit—*which are unseen*.

The things we do today will make the manner of individual we will be tomorrow or a million years from now. We don't die to be in eternity: we are already in it! Then it's just as important to understand whence we came, as it is to understand where we are going. To know whence we came is to know what we're up against. If we use the abilities we have, we will be given more tomorrow. The next step to take will be given us.

It is self-exaltation and it is selfishness that carry us away from the knowledge of God. These bring doubts, fears, and all those qualities *bespeaking the visible* or making for worry, hardship and misunderstanding.

Whatever may be troubling us, let us take it to God, to Christ. We will be shown the way.

February 26, 1933

THE SECOND COMING

Edgar Cayce

This is a subject about which very little is known. Jesus Himself said that it was given only to the Father to know the time of His return. We have, however, two sources of information from which we will draw material to use in forming our ideas about this subject. We will turn to the Bible for part of our discussion, and secondly we will consider information we have received psychically, which may clarify the various passages.

First, I would like to define the word *psychic*. Do not get the idea that psychic information means what Uncle John has to say, or Aunt Sue—though it might mean that to some people, at this time. Rather, let us consider the meaning from a broader angle as it relates to the development and use of the *soul faculties*. Also, let me assure you that I have reason for the faith that lies within me—a faith which may or may not seem orthodox to you.

First, then, what does the Master say about the second coming? How has anyone gotten the idea that there is to be a second coming? It is mentioned in John 14: 1-3: "Jesus said, Let not your heart be troubled; ye believe in God, believe also in me . . . And if I go and prepare a place for you, I will come again, and receive you unto myself; that where I am, there ye may be also."

When we look into the history of the world as we know it today, how often has a great religious leader or prophet arisen? Plato said that our cycle of entering is about every thousand years. Judging from history itself, the period of time between each religious teacher who has come into the earth varies from six hundred and twenty five years to twelve hundred.

Do you ask, "Is that how often you say Christ has come?" No, I don't say that; I don't know how many times He has come; however, if we will consider the following passages of Scripture for a few moments, an interesting idea may be formulated. These are the passages: (See John 1: 1-14)

"In the beginning was the Word, and the Word was with God, and the Word was God. The same was in the beginning with God. All things were made by him; and without him was not anything made that was made . . . And the Word was made flesh, and dwelt among us . . . He was in the world, and the world was made by him, and the world knew him not."

Many people tell us that this is speaking of spiritual things. You must answer this for yourself. But if the Word was made flesh and dwelt among men, how can we be sure that this is not speaking materially, too?

In talking with those who should have been and were the judges of Israel at that time, the Master said:

"I know that ye are Abraham's seed; but ye seek to kill me, because my word hath no place in you . . . If ye were Abraham's children, ye would do the works of Abraham . . . Ye are of your father the devil . . ." (John 8: 37-44)

In the flesh, yes, they were the children of Abraham, but in spirit they were not. For what did Abraham do? He

25

was righteous, and his deeds were counted to him for righteousness because of his faith in the One God.

In this same chapter, the Master said, "Your father Abraham rejoiced to see my day, and he saw it, and was glad." Then said the Jews unto Him. "Thou art not yet fifty years old, and hast thou seen Abraham?" Jesus said unto them, "Verily, verily I say unto you, before Abraham was, *I am.*"

Did Jesus mean that in a spiritual sense or a literal sense—or both? What do you think? I don't know, but what we have been told psychically is this—take it for what it is worth, and *apply it in your own experience.*

Now turn to the fourteenth Chapter of Genesis and read where Abraham paid tribute to a certain individual, Melchizedek. No cause or reason is given except that the man came out in the place to bless him: a priest of the Most High God, without days, a man not born normally but a high priest of the living God. "And Melchizedek, king of Salem, brought forth bread and wine; and he was the priest of the most high God. And he blessed him . . . "

Was this the Master, this Melchizedek? I don't know. Read it yourself. Maybe I'm wrong in thinking it was the Master, the man we know later as Jesus.

Consider now the book of Joshua. Who directed Joshua when he became the leader of Israel? Who walked out to lead Joshua after he crossed the Jordan? The Bible says, the Son of Man. The Son of Man came out to lead the armies of the Lord. And after Joshua's experience in meeting this man of God, all of the children of Israel were afraid of him. (See Joshua 5: 13-15.)

From the above references, let us draw a few conclusions and supplement them with psychic information. The Spirit of the Christ manifested in the earth many times before the coming of Jesus; at times it manifested through one like Melchizedek, and at other times it manifested as a spiritual influence through some teacher upholding the worship of the One God.

What has this conclusion to do with the second coming? Well, in the light of the above, there ceases to be a *second* coming. Also by considering conditions that made His appearance possible at various times—or, if you prefer, the one time as Jesus—we can deduce certain facts about the return of the Master.

How did He happen to come as Jesus of Nazareth? There had not been a revelation to man, of which we have any record, for over four hundred years. Then did darkness and dissipation on the part of man bring Christ into the world? If so, it is a reversal of the natural law, *Like begets Like*. The laws of God are not reversed at any time and never will we find them so. They are immutable and hold true throughout any kingdom we may find in the earth. The things we see developing in the various kingdoms in this earth are merely shadows of the celestial and terrestrial world. For we grow in grace and knowledge and understanding, as another Bible writer has said. By what *means* comes growth? By *application* of truths in our lives.

Then what brought about the coming of Jesus? A people who were sincere seekers—a little group founded for the purpose of seeking to make themselves channels whereby this great thing could come to pass. Who were these people? They were the most hated of all those mentioned in profane history, and scarcely mentioned in the Bible—the Essenes, the hated ones, the lowest of the Jews.

You may ask how we can know this. We have received it psychically, yes; and hundreds of others have. But how many more times was Zacharias allowed to go up and offer sacrifices, after being spoken to once, within the temple? Never again! For he had joined that hated group, and thereby made his son—who by lineal descent was a high priest—an outcast. Who was the cousin of Elizabeth? Mary, the mother of Him we worship as our Lord and Master. Mary sought first her cousin Elizabeth, the mother of the great Essene, John the Baptist, to tell the great tidings that the angel had made known to her.

These Essenes, then, were consecrating and dedicating their lives, their inner selves, to make possible a meeting place for God and man; with such a spiritual degree of consecration that Jesus the Christ might come into the world. Thus there was a *preparation*, where there might be the meeting place for God and man. And if we will have a meeting place in our heart, our home, our group, our church, then we too can have the Christ come to us. When

27

we have prepared the place, He will come—and not before.

We can't say that we are diligently seeking but He has gone to somebody else. It isn't common sense. We can't say that somebody else has to prepare the way for us. He will come again, yes; and He will come as He is. His spirit is here always. It will abide with us always.

In no place where the Master taught was he accepted, and he taught in Palestine, Egypt, India, Persia, China, Japan—at least in all those places.

We all believe that He descended into hell and taught those there. We read it in the Bible and we say it is true. But we don't really believe it, else we would act like it! If we did believe it, we would never find fault with any soul in the world—never! For if we believe that He went into hell and taught the people there, how could we find fault with our next door neighbor because his chickens got into our garden or because he doesn't believe exactly as we do?

Is this in your Bible: "Moreover I will endeavor that ye may be able after my decease to have these things always in remembrance." (II Peter 1: 15) Did you ever hear a sermon preached on it? The man who said that is the one of whom Christ said, "Flesh and blood hath not revealed this unto thee, but my Father in heaven." To the same man, perhaps only a few minutes afterwards, He said, "Get thee behind me, Satan: thou art an offense unto me: for thou savourest not the things that be of God, but those that be of men"—the things of the flesh and not the things of the spirit. (Matt. 16: 23)

The master said, "Elias truly shall come first, and restore all things. But I say unto you, that Elias is come already, and they knew him not, but have done unto him whatsoever they listed. Likewise shall also the Son of man suffer of them. Then the disciples understood that He spake unto them of John the Baptist." (Matt. 17: 11-13)

Possibly you may say that He meant in the spirit and not in the flesh; but I don't read it that way.

A warning was once given to a man of God that a certain country would be destroyed; but the man prayed and talked with God face to face, and God promised that if there were fifty righteous men he would save it. Then

28

finally, if there were just ten righteous men He would spare the city.

I believe that the just people in the world keep it going. The just people are the ones who have been kind to the other fellow. For we may see evidences of the Christ Spirit about us right now, day by day: in kindness, patience, long-suffering, showing brotherly love, preferring our neighbor before ourselves. When there are possibly fifty, or a hundred, or a thousand, or million—then the way may have been prepared for His coming. But all these just men must have *united* in their desire and supplication that the Christ physically walk among men again.

He for our sakes became flesh. How many times? Answer for yourself. How soon will He come again? When we make it possible. It was made possible at least once. It will be made possible again. When we live the life He has laid out for us, we are making it possible for Him, the Lord and Master of this world, to come again.

"I will not leave you comfortless, but I will come again, and receive you unto myself, that where I am, there ye may be also."

May 7, 1934

WHAT IS TRUTH?

Edgar Cayce

We have spoken on various subjects from Sunday to Sunday. From time to time I have been speaking of the things that have had to do principally with the material things of life—or have *to do* with the material—putting them in such a way and manner that we may be able to use them in our everyday life.

As I have said, I am going to try to talk to you this afternoon about Truth—or "What Is Truth?"

I realize I am assuming a big job. I've read very little of

the philosophers of the ages. Yet we know that throughout the ages there has been the continual cry of *"What Is Truth?"*

We often hear it said that Truth is evasive—Truth is naked—Truth will not be downed; but what is Truth?

We remember, if we turn to the books of the New Testament, that possibly the greatest moment in history was when Pilate asked of the Master "What is truth?" Possibly that was the *only* time it could have been answered in one or two words, that would have at least satisfied the greater portion of the thinking world today. But Pilate did not wait for the answer. Yet we know that the Master said He *came* that He might show the way unto Truth. All right. Then we know Truth is something that we may be *shown*.

When we speak of *a* truth, or *the* truth, or *Truth,* possibly we mean different things. You will remember, those of you who have read the little story—and I'm sure most of you have—of the three men of Hindustan who went to see the elephant, but all three men were blind. Now that's us—we are all blind! Yet we are seeking the truth, and we are very much in the same position as those three men who went to see the elephant. One of these stumbled against the side of the elephant, and he said, "I perceive, without a doubt, the elephant is very like a wall." Wasn't that the truth to him? Another one, as he stumbled about, found the elephant's trunk and said, "I perceive with a certainty that the elephant is very like a tree." The third man, as he stumbled about, got hold of the tail and he said, "I perceive the elephant is very much like a rope."

Now were they in error? Did they have *the* truth? Or did they have only a portion of the truth? Did they have any of the truth?

We often say that any movement, of any character, succeeds in so far as it has a portion of the truth. We may be sure *that's* truth. Then don't worry because you disagree with any individual as to what your conception of any movement may be—don't think anyone is going to hell because he doesn't think as you do! Remember the three blind men who went to see the elephant! Just *know* that people may be right, but wrong as *you* would see it, with your eyes wide open.

Life in its projection into this material plane has been a constant growth. Then if we are to believe the things that have been presented to us—and *as they are presented to us*—we know that even Truth itself may be a *growth into* that understanding which we will be able to apply in our everyday life.

I am sure we believe God is Love. Our love for a person, then, is an expression of the force, or manifested force, that we define as Love. Here was an experience that came to a man. He was very much in love with his wife. He thought more of her than anything in the world, but God saw fit to take her home; and when the man erected a monument in the cemetery, he had this inscribed on it: *"The light of my life has gone out."* He couldn't find anything that could reconcile him about his separation, until after a while he met a young lady he fell very much in love with and then he found that he was altogether mistaken about his first love being able to satisfy everything in his life! There was something else that had been added—he had gained the knowledge of someone else being able to fill up a portion of his life.

The young lady, knowing about this inscription, said to him, "I might consent to be your wife, but I don't think I could ever do that as long as the inscription remains as it is." So he went about to find a man who could correct this for him; and when the man who had charge of such things told him he saw how he could rectify this inscription, he went ahead with the wedding. When they came back from their honeymoon, they went out to see how it read and this is what they found: "The light of my life has gone out—but I've struck another match."

So you see there are individual experiences of truth. When we read or get an idea of some particular thought or some particular rule, we gradually build into our own selves an idea that we have gotten *the whole thing!*

Now is Truth such a thing that those who have been followers of Mohammed have *all of the truth?* Have those who have been the followers of Moses, the law-givers, all of the truth? Or hasn't it been, rather, a growth in our individual lives; and what may be truth for one individual may not, in the experience of another individual, answer at all? Does that make the other any less true for the other individual? Did this man love the second woman any less, from his experience of being in love before?

Then if this be true, it is possible that truth is a changeable thing—is a growth. Will it be possible for us to find something of which we can say *"This is Truth"* and know that it will answer in everything or in every way that life may present itself to us?

I believe that we can. You may differ with me. I don't think, however, that you will be able to refute what will be my definition, or what I will be able to say is *Truth*. Many of you will say, "Well, have you been given some peculiar power, that you have knowledge of what Truth is?" Let's see if this will not answer the whole question in our lives.

First, we must know that if we are to accept any word or any follower as a truth—or the truth, or Truth—we must be sure of the *authority* that we quote. We must be very sure of our foundation, or platform, for what we have assumed. Where would we begin, as we would say, in assuming something as being true?

We must recognize these facts in our lives: there is a physical body, there is a spiritual body. We know the physical body is dependent upon its physical attributes for its development. It is also the temple or the dwelling place of the spiritual body. The spiritual body, we know, is of the Creator—whatever we may call the Creator. It comes from the same thing, even if we go back to scientific reasoning and say it begins from the lowest form of life. Wherever we begin, we have to say there is something beyond that, where it has developed—whether you believe in evolution, creative evolution, or what not. All reasoning has to go back to the very same thing, and if I can answer this at all, I don't believe I'm wrong in saying that you can reason from any standpoint you want to take—but *this is Truth*:

That which, kept before your mental mind, your spiritual mind, will continue to develop you upward!

Now, let's see if this applies to any of the phases that may present themselves, and answers any of the questions you would want to ask. That which, held before your mental vision, will *continue* to develop you upward! Not that

32

which satisfies selfish purpose, no! Not that which tells you whether it is wrong to go fishing on Sunday or not, or to play baseball on Sunday. Not that which answers such questions. It furnishes answers, yes—but that which will continue to develop you upward.

All right, then: what do we mean by developing upward? That which will enable you to hold the vision of what *you* worship as *your* God.

Every man, every individual, every object has its conception of its superior position. We would ask, then, "Well, would it answer the Indian who is looking for his Happy Hunting Ground?" Why wouldn't it answer? That which will enable him to hold before him what *he* worships as *his* God is Truth, to him.

Now, what have we assumed or taken for granted? We have taken for granted that man has a mind, that man has a body—a physical body, and a spiritual body. He has a soul, if you please! His soul, or his spiritual body, is controlled by his subconscious or his spiritual mind. Whatever continues to hold before the individual that which he worships as his God will continue, then, to develop the individual *towards* that which he worships. Then you will say, "What would have been the Master's answer to Pilate's question?" Would it not be, "I came into the world to do no other than conduct you into that which is Truth."

Truth, then, is not a thing that we can see or perceive with the ears or body senses; but Truth is the essence with which an individual builds faith, hope and trust. That is Truth, that essence which we are enabled to hold before our mental vision.

Will it build your body? *It will!* Will it heal the sick? *It will!*

A few days ago I was talking to some people and they told me about a book that had been written by some of the masters from the Far East. I had never seen the book before, but when I opened it to read it, I knew what was in it before I read it. I don't know how, nor why—but I knew the experiences I was going to encounter. Within the first four or five pages, I found that in this book one thought was stressed: what you hold before yourself, to create that image you worship—that is what will develop you always upward, and will continue to enable you to know truth.

33

Truth, then, being a growing thing; truth, being a thing that will develop you; is a something that is *entirely in action!* That's what God is! For in every *movement* that has ever been, there has been a continual upward development—upward toward that which is Truth.

If you hold malice, you can become one of the meanest persons in the world. You know that if you continue to send out thought (which may become a miracle or a crime), you create those very same cross-currents in your own mind. What is prayer but simply attuning yourself to that which you are seeking assistance through? That's all prayer is—the attunement to that very same thing; and *that becomes Truth when it becomes an action.* When it goes into action, to you it becomes Truth. It's your own conception of what your God is. If it makes you better in relationship to the very thing you worship—if it makes you more in accord with what you worship—then that is what you become, whether it's downward or upward. You go whichever way your standard is set.

Now as to who is to say whether you are building up—or how near it brings you to what you worship as your God (because *God is Truth*): whatever you continue to hold, you develop toward. Someone else whose God might be something else, wouldn't find this to be his Truth.

I've been studying a long while, trying to understand what is meant by the second commandment, and I never did understand what it meant until the other night—that is, satisfactorily, in my own mind. The first commandment, as we know, is "Thou shalt love the Lord thy God with all thy heart and thy mind, etc." The second is "Thou shalt not make unto thee any graven image."

Why not? Because if you make an image, it becomes your God. But if you have for your God that which is within your own individual self—you yourself being a portion of the Creator—you will continue to build upward, to it!

1929 or early 1930

34

MAN'S RELATIONSHIP TO GOD

Edgar Cayce

Please understand that I am not trying to explain your relationship to God. I am only hoping that I will be able to tell you something that will stimulate you to thought.

First it is necessary that we review, as we might say, man's experience in the earth's plane—as far as we have a history of it. The broadest understanding that we can get, I think, is from the Scripture itself. I don't mean that I am going to preach any special theology or even give you an idea of what I believe in the theology of the day, or the theology of the past.

It doesn't matter what we may claim to believe. What is really worthwhile is what difference does what we believe make in our lives? What change or difference does a belief make that comes into your life? That's the thing people are really interested in. The world doesn't care whether you believe the whale swallowed Jonah, or whether Noah was in the Ark a whole year or only forty days. What is an individual's belief in those things that have come into his life—that has changed his attitude toward his fellow man or towards his God? This is important.

If we take the history given us in the Bible, we would begin with the first individual who, we find, had a concept of his relation to God. Who would this first man be? Not Adam; no, for Adam's concept at first was his relationship to his fellow man, or his relationship to his mate—if we consider him just as an individual. It is the seventh from Adam who, we find, had a different concept entirely. "Now Enoch walked with God and he was not, for God took him."

Enoch was considered by the people of that day as a man with an individuality. Enoch, we find, was one who began to consider his relationship to his Creator—call

Him by what you will, whether the God of the First cause, the God of nature, or the God of the divine. It changed that man's life.

The next man we find who comes down through history as one who had a definite religious experience is Noah. Now, Noah was a *just* man. He was a perfect man in his day and generation, but his experience changed his attitude—not only as to his relationship to what he worshipped as his God but as to his relationship to individuals around him—and it brought a different activity in his life.

Abraham is the next. His experience brought to the world a great change. He was called out to make of his seed and of his generation a peculiar people, a separate and distinct nation. He was an elderly man without an offspring, yet God spoke to him and made him a great promise. "Now separate yourself from among these people and go out to a strange land which I will give to your seed forever as a heritage. I will make of you a peculiar people, and through your seed will all the nations of the earth be blessed." Abraham harkened to that call.

In this very matter there lies for most of us a great fault. Have any of us so lived that we were called to do a special thing? Have any of us so lived that we may be guided by that something from within that will direct us if we would but stop to harken to "the Voice"? We notice that when this call came to Abraham, he heard the call and knew it was not in *him* that the people were to be blessed, but in the way that he was to act towards his brethren. He was to separate himself from these for a peculiar service.

This idea has grown to seed. This is held against those very people. They separated themselves from others as a chosen people of God. It was to make a nation that Abraham was called, and through Abraham *all* nations should be blessed. Through the acts of this individual, through his understanding and response to the call, all people were to find happiness. But when these people began to make this promise an individual thing, that "I can sin because I am chosen," they began to fall by the way.

Next we come to Isaac. When the day came for him to be taken to his fathers, he called about him his twelve sons and explained to each his faults and virtues. He showed

36

them what each, through his concept of his relationship to Jehovah, had built and was building—and that to which it would come in their lives. All that he told them came to pass.

The next in line is Moses, who was raised up to be a deliverer of his people. Abraham had been told that his seed would be in bondage for four hundred years, and then one would be raised up who would lead them back to this promised land which he himself was not allowed to possess; but which would become the land of his people, For He would remain to them a God if they would remain to Him a people. There is something that man must do, as well as something that the Creator must do. There is a purpose in life—it is not a haphazard thing.

Now we come down to the days when the Jews went out to the promised land. As they wandered through the wilderness they began to think about their own personal relationship to God. They forgot all the hardships through which they had passed in Egypt. Human nature has always been—and will always be—just the same. As we pass through life, we feel that the present is about the hardest time we have ever had, but after a few years have passed we begin to look back on those things and see only what has come out of this. Why does this happen? There is a reason. When the people murmured and when they asked that they might have a physical God, that they might see something that was tangible, they cried to Moses: "You speak of the spirit and you are able to go up on the mountain and bring us wonderful messages, but we don't see Him, we don't hear Him. We hear only those things that you come back and tell us. We have seen the pillar of fire by night and the cloud by day—but these have become everyday matters. We expect these. Now we want to do things that other people do. We want a God like they have."

They had forgotten they were called out to be a separate and distinct nation. They had forgotten the call that had come to their forefathers, and the heritage they were about to claim.

Throughout all of this, Moses maintained his faith in, and upheld, the God he had come to know through personal experiences. He had heard the call from within. God

37

to him had become a personal God. For the people who fought among themselves at the foot of the mountains, God was still the God of war—the God with the big stick who beat off their enemies but would turn on them if they went too far.

Can't we get his idea: *God is a personal God!* He is not a God of war or a God of plenty—nor even a God of an individual. He is a God of all; in all things; and our heritage is in Him. We may illustrate this: Just as the earthly parent feels in respect to his own children, so may we in our own selves conceive of *something* that God may feel, must feel, about His children, His people here in this world.

It is His purpose that we make ourselves a channel through which His spirit may manifest. He would use us.

We may be the channel through which the other fellow, less fortunate than we, may be aided in whatever is needed for him to gain a better conception of his relationship to His God.

It would be well if we could all remember the decision of the great Jewish leader who said, "Others may do as they may, but for me and my house, we will worship the living God." Daily we are confronted with problems that require just such a definite stand. Let us remember His promise and be strong.

We may now trace the history of the Jews on down to the time when the first king was chosen. Saul was raised up to be their king and leader, yet he failed to understand that the time had come when the people had developed to the point where God did not desire a sacrifice of animals, but of individuals, to His cause.

David was the next in line and despite the fact that he did many things that we today call sins, we may learn many lessons from his attitude toward his god. Saul tried many times to kill him yet always David said, "It is not meet that I should raise mine hand against an anointed of the Lord." It is not right that one individual should raise his voice against another individual who is doing his service in the manner he feels God has spoken to him.

Finally there comes the last rise to power. The Jewish nation became under King Solomon, David's son, one of the greatest of the time. After the beautiful temple had been built and prosperity came to the nation, the people began to forget their relationship to God; and led by the king they turned to the worship of the physical pleasures of the world. Their fall is near. The period of the prophets follows. Individuals arose who had a vision of what the relationship to God should be, but the people would not listen to them and the Jews were torn apart as a nation, and scattered to the four winds.

This question has come down to every age, to every individual: *What is your relationship to your God?* It came to Enoch, to Noah, to Abraham, to Isaac, to Moses, to Joshua, to Saul, to David, to Solomon—and it comes just the same to you today. What is your relationship to Him? Remember that He is the God of the Living, not of the dead. Remember that in serving Him you must serve your fellow man; that you must become a channel through which God may work His divine will here on earth.

When the burdens become hard to bear and you feel yourself beginning to slip away from the path you know is right, draw nearer to your God and He will draw nearer to you. As a child will come and sit at the feet of its parents, seeking their guidance and advice, asking their help; just so we must approach through prayer the God who is our Father and Creator.

Now in coming to know Him, is it not evident that as we consider and help our fellow man, so do we carry out God's work? Our relationship to our God then becomes our relationship to our brother. There is nothing that we can do for God, but there is much that we can do for His Children, His created creatures—our brothers. As we go about in our everyday work, let us remember to lend a helping hand wherever we may—and know that in so doing, we are fulfilling the Will of the Creator, and coming ever nearer to our God.

1929 or early 1930

PEACE IN OUR TIME

Violet M. Shelley

Across the country the prayers of a troubled people petition for peace. Letters to congressmen, to editors of newspapers and magazines, echo the cry. Demonstrations reflect the widespread wish. In recent years the lack of peace and the threat of the hydrogen bomb have been held accountable for juvenile delinquency, drug addiction, and most recently for the destructive riots that have erupted in the ghettoes of our large cities. The thoughtful person has often had cause to ask himself "Where are we headed?" and "What can I do?"

Dr. Laurence M. Gould, famous geologist, Antarctic expert, and President Emeritus of Carleton College in Northfield, Minnesota, wrote:

"I do not believe the greatest threat to our future is from bombs or guided missiles. I don't think our civilization will die that way. I think it will die when we no longer care—when the spiritual forces that make us wish to be right and noble die in the hearts of men. Arnold Toynbee has pointed out that 19 of 21 notable civilizations have died from within and not by conquest from without. There were no bands playing and no flags waving when these civilizations decayed; it happened slowly, in the quiet and the dark when no one was aware. . . .

"If America is to grow great, we must stop gagging at the word 'spiritual.' Our task is to rediscover and reassert our faith in the spiritual, nonutilitarian values on which American life has really rested from its beginning." *

* Reprinted from THIS WEEK magazine. Copyright 1959 by the United Newspapers Magazine Corporation.

The information in the telepathic-clairvoyant readings of the late Edgar Cayce affirmed the necessity for spiritual purpose and direction. The readings point over and over to the fact that man is a spiritual being, and the series of readings taken on the "work" of the Association for Research and Enlightenment emphasize that this organization must also be spiritual in purpose and direction. If this is so, if man is created in the image of God—that is, in spirit, what has he to do with and about the chaos in the world today?

In the beginning when chaos existed in the creating of the earth, the Spirit of God moved over the face of same and out of chaos came the world—with its beauty in natural form, or in nature.

With man's advent into the world, then personalities, individualities, began to find expressions in *subduing* the earth, and man—with his natural bent—not only attempted to subdue the *earth,* but to subdue one another; and the result was the difference of opinions, the various sects, sets, classes and races . . .

. . . With the advent of the closeness of the worlds coming into being, so that the man upon the other side of the world is as much the neighbor as the man next door, more and more have been the turmoils that have arisen in the attempt of individual leaders or groups to induce, force or compel, one portion of the world to think as the other, or the other group to dwell together as brethren with one bond of sympathy, or one standard for all.

With the present conditions, then, that exist— these have all come to that place in the development of the human family where there must be a reckoning, a one point upon which all may agree, that out of all of this turmoil that has risen from the social life,

41

racial differences, the outlook upon the relationship of man to the Creative Forces or his God, and his relationships one with another, must come the same *common* basis upon which all *may* agree. You say at once, such a thing is impractical, impossible! What has caused the present conditions, not alone at home but abroad? It is that realization that was asked some thousands of years ago, "Where *is* thy brother? His blood *cries* to me from the ground!" and the other portion of the world has answered, *is* answering, "Am I my brother's keeper?" The world, *as* a world—that makes for the disruption, for the discontent—has lost its ideal. Man may not have the same *idea.* Man—*all* men—may have the *same* IDEAL!

As the Spirit of God once moved to bring peace and harmony out of chaos, so must the Spirit move over the earth and magnify itself in the hearts, minds and souls of men to bring peace, harmony and understanding, that they may dwell together in a way that will bring that peace, that harmony, that can only come with all having the *one Ideal;* not the one *idea,* but "Thou shalt love the Lord Thy God with all thine heart, thy neighbor as thyself!" This is the whole law, this is the whole answer to the world, to each and every soul. That is the answer to the world conditions as they exist today.   3976-8

And so, as the Spirit of God once moved across the face of the earth, we are told that it must once again move over the earth if we are to dwell in peace, harmony, and understanding. What does this mean to us? If we are in fact spiritual by nature and if our purposes and desires are spiritual then we are entitled to a great hope. The readings Edgar Cayce gave on World Affairs allude very often to the story of Abraham pleading with the Lord and extracting the promise that if there were ten righteous men within the city of Sodom it would not be destroyed. (Genesis 18)

In 1932, the Biblical reference took on personal meaning.

A-4. Europe is as a house broken up. Some years ago there was the experience of a mighty people being overridden for the gratification and satisfaction of a few, irrespective of any other man's right. These people are going through the experience of being born *again*—a thorn in the flesh to many a political and financial nation in Europe, in the world—but out of same, with the prayers and supplications of those that may pray—even as Abraham—"If there be fifty, will it not be spared?" "O, if there be ten faithful, will it not be spared?" Then, the hope of Europe depends upon *YOU!* in your own home TODAY! In not the same *way,* but the same *manner* as did the life of Lot, or of the other people in Sodom and Gomorrah.   3976-8

So, in the experience of those that have sent and made the conditions are greed, selfishness; that has been practiced in the minds, in the lives, in the experience of the nation. Think not any soul, "Yea, that is true for the other fellow." But it applies to Jim, to Tom, to those in ordinary walks of life, to those who have been given those powers in high places, those that have wealth about them; *they* are the oppressors; yea, look within thine own heart! Hast thou not practiced the same? For, as it has been given, "Yea, though there be only ten just men, they may save the city; they may save the nation; they may save the world," if they will but *practice* in their daily experience that which has been the command from the first: "Thou shalt love the Lord thy God with all thine heart, and thy neighbor as thyself."

This the basis of all *spiritual* law; and to you would there be given as this:

There is no activity in the experience of man that has not its inception or purpose in the spirit of those injunctions but what *must* fail; unless it is founded in the spirit of truth.

Hence each would ask, then: "What must *I* do about it? not what shall this, that or the other ruler, other

43

office holder, or the other individual do," but each should ask, "What must *I* do about the economic conditions in which we find ourselves?"

So live each day, each hour, as to put into practice those precepts, those influences in thine own life, and in the life of all ye contact day by day. For, He hath said, "Though ye wander far afield, if ye will cry unto me, if ye will ask, if ye will draw unto me, I will draw nigh unto thee; and my help, my arm is not short as man's counting of shortness, but will bring to thee speedily that which is the desire of thine heart, if it is conceived in righteousness.   3976-14

These readings reaffirm the story of the Lord's promise to Abraham, and emphasize the importance of the truly spiritual man. They point out, however, that the importance lies not with conversation about spiritual law, but with the individual's adherence to that law in his daily life.

Can prayer help? Surely earnest and sincere prayers go heavenward across the whole nation. Why can they not be answered speedily? The information in the Cayce readings assures us of the value of prayer, and of its power to bring about peace. There are, however, certain requirements of the petitioner for peace, and each of us on noting those requirements needs to examine himself honestly.

These, then, with the necessary preparedness for the meeting of all emergencies in ANY direction that may be taken by those who allow their hates and their disputes to overcome or to put aside brotherly love.

For it is as brother against brother in the disputes.

And know that all stand as one before the judgement bar of the Creator.

Hence prayer, and more prayer; and as we have given, LIVE toward one another as a nation, as a brother nation to the others—on EITHER side—as ye pray!

Do not pray one way and live another! Be consistent, be persistent.   3976-20

Hence we find at this present time, NOW, the conditions or the circumstances throughout the nations of

44

the world, or in the earth, are a challenge to every thinking person; that ye are not alone to pray for peace but are to PURSUE peace—by LIVING the second phase of the divine injunction, "thy neighbor as thyself."

Then today, we are to answer within our individual consciousness, "Am I my brother's keeper?.. Not "What does the world owe me?" but "What contribution can *I*, as an individual soul seeking God, seeking to know His face, make that may hasten the day of the Lord?"

For we as individuals, as we look about us, realize more and more that indeed we live and move and have our being in Him—and we are becoming mindful also of "from whence we came." And we realize that as He has given, "If ye will be my people, I will be thy God" applies to me, to you, to each soul that has been blessed with the consciousness, the awareness of life.

For Life itself in all its forms and phases is indeed a manifestation of that we worship as God.

We realize that selfishness, jealousies, those things that make people afraid must gradually be put away.

First, then, as an individual, self must be conquered. Rather than raising thy voice, then, that YE may be heard, raise thy voice that HE, thy God may be heard!

WHO, then, is thy God? Is it thyself, thy body, thy ego? Rather look, then, to Him who is able to keep you from falling, but is able to keep you in strength of His might by thy desire, thy purpose, thy aims being "Others, Lord! Others!"   3976-22

Then, there needs be that not so much be set as to this ritual, or this form, or the other, for any given peoples or any nation, but rather that the individuals in each nation, EVERYWHERE, are to turn again TO the God of the fathers and not in self-indulgence, self-aggrandizement, but more and more of self-effacement.

For as the people of each nation pray, AND then live that prayer, so must the Spirit work.

Then—each of you here—GIVE GOD A
45

CHANCE to show what great blessings He will give to those who love Him. This does not mean that ye, or ANYONE, would condone persecutions anywhere or in any form. For, know ye, His laws fail not—"As ye sow, so shall ye reap."

Man can only begin, then, within himself. And as he applies that he knows, that he understands of God, in his daily life, so may there be given him the next step to make . . .

. . . "What then," ye ask, "is to be the outcome? What is there that I can do about it?"

Let thy daily life be free from criticism, from condemnation, from hate, from jealousy. And as ye give power to the Spirit of Peace, so may the PRINCE OF PEACE, the love of God, manifest.

So long as ye turn thy thoughts to the manners and means for meeting and overcoming those destructive forces, ye show forth that which may bring to the world that day of the lord. For the promise is that in the latter days there shall be the purposes in the HEARTS of men, everywhere!   3976-23

When there has been in the earth those groups that have sufficiently desired and sought peace, peace will begin. It must be within self.   3976-28

. . . Then, we find, peace in the world must begin first within the heart and purpose and mind of the individual, prompted by that something which answers within—even as has been given, "My spirit beareth witness with thy spirit, as to whether ye be the children of God or not."

As man looks upon the world today, there comes that understanding, that manner in which choice and judgments may be drawn; even as He gave to that one who had announced by the authority of the prophets, "Behold the lamb of God, that taketh away the sins of the world," who comes to bring peace into the hearts of those who seek to do righteousness in the earth. And yet because he had fallen into that answering as to self to fears within, he began to doubt—as apparently no measure was being attempted, outwardly at least, to relieve him of his bonds, and he asked, "Art thou He that was to come, or shall we look for another?" The Master's answer is the judgment of today, even as then. There was not the Yes or the No answer, but "Go tell John that the sick are healed, the poor have the gospel preached, the lame walk, the blind see."

Not merely the physically lame, not merely the physically blind, not merely the physically sick—but it was that which answered to the whole purpose of man's experience in the earth, which was completed in Him; that makes it possible for as many as believe to become the children of the living God.

Then, thinkest thou that ye can treat thy neighbor, thy brother, with aught but the spirit of truth, the fruits of the spirit that He gave, and find other than that ye measure out? For, with what measure ye mete it is measured to thee again. As ye do it unto the least ye do it unto thy Maker.

Whose spirit, what manner of peace, then, seek ye as individuals? That ye may gratify the appetites of thy body? That ye may satisfy the lust of the eye? That ye may know fame or fortune? These fade, these pass away.

Only that which enables the individual also to bear the cross, even as He, will enable that individual to know that peace which encompassed Him in such a measure that He broke the bonds of death, overcame hell and the grave, and rose in a newness of life; that ye—here—and now—might know that peace in these troubled periods.   3976-27

What CAN you do, then, as individuals, that this plague of war, this injustice to man be taken away—this plague of death and fear of destruction?

YE MAY STAND—EVEN AS HE—BETWEEN THE LIVING AND THE DEAD!

Let those that die have that purpose even as He, "It shall NOT BE IN VAIN!"

Let those that live LIVE unto God; magnifying, spreading the fruits of brotherly love, kindness, patience; that this plague of war may be stayed.

Ye cannot pray "Peace—Peace" when there is no peace in thine own heart and soul! but by knowing (for His spirit answers with thy spirit) that each day, each person ye meet is GLAD that you are alive! GLAD that YOU have come in touch with them; for you have brought—and bring—hope to their lives, just in the passing!

This means, then, that you may so live the life as He emulated in the earth, that ye radiate life, joy, peace! that which casteth out fear—by living, by being, by doing unto others, for others, that ye would like others to do unto you.

Oh, ye say, this is not new! Neither is thy present disturbance, nor thy present hope, nor ANYTHING! For, even as he said, "There is nothing new under the sun." What is has been, and will be again. Only as ye USE that birthright, that purpose, that WILL within thine own consciousness to do justice, to do right, to LOVE good, to eschew evil, may ye as individuals, as a group, as a nation, stand between the living and the dead—and STAY the sin that maketh man make war—of any nature—against his brother.

Thou ART thy brother's keeper! Act that in thine own heart. Who IS thy brother? "Who is my mother? They that do the will of the Father, the same is my mother, my sister, my brother."

If ye do the things of the devil, are ye not his? If ye do the things of the Lord (He is God), are ye not His?

Then study to show thyself approved unto God, a workman not ashamed, rightly dividing the words of truth, keeping SELF unspotted from the world. In this ye may build, here a little, there a little, line upon line, precept upon precept.

Fear and doubt cast away, trusting in the Lord. He alone can save.   3976-27

There is nothing of superstitious ritual in these suggestions, nor is there panacea for the faint of heart. Can we face the inference that the onus lies with us, individually? Do we really want peace enough to do something in our own lives? The requirement set forth so clearly is that we start with ourselves. If we are not willing to do that we must content ourselves with wringing our hands, lamenting the idiocy of war, and hoping that someone else will care enough to cause peace to prevail.

A reading given in June of 1940 for the Ninth Annual Congress of the Association for Research and Enlightenment, pointed up dramatically the power of a group who were united in sincerity and dedication. The big "if" is still there. Those gathered for the Congress were told that *were* they to *live* their prayer, they *could* save America from being invaded.

Let thy voice be raised, then, as in praise to thy Maker; not in word alone but rather in the manner in which ye meet thy fellow men day by day. For the prayer, and the living of same by those sixty and four who are here gathered, may even save America from being invaded—if that is what ye desire.

For the Lord CAN, the Lord WILL, the Lord DOES preserve those who in RIGHTEOUSNESS ask. "Ask and ye shall receive; knock and it shall be opened unto you."

And as ye live, so may the Christian light of LOVE encompass the earth; not that of hate, selfishness, money, power, or fame!

Then, all ye who are gathered here—Do not entrust this to someone else, but "I—even I!" Let rather thy cry be: "LORD, HERE AM I! USE ME IN THE WAY AND MANNER THAT THOU SEEST BEST FIT; THAT WE MAY PRESERVE THE FAITH WE HAVE IN THE LORD, THE SAVIOR, JESUS THE CHRIST; THAT WE MAY STILL BE AS ONE BROTHERHOOD; AS ONE KNOWING THOU ART NEAR; AS ONE MANIFESTING THY POWER, O GOD; NOT OF OURSELVES, BUT THAT OTHERS MAY SEE THY GLORY—EVEN THE ONE NEXT TO ME. EVEN THOUGH HE MAY CURSE, MAY SWEAR, MAY DO THOSE THINGS THAT ARE UNSEEMLY, LET THY POWER BE MANIFESTED, O GOD; THAT JESUS, THY SON,

MAY INDEED COME INTO THE EARTH;
THAT ALL MEN MAY KNOW THAT HE IS
THE LORD OF MY HEART, MY MIND, MY
BODY, MY HOME, MY COUNTY, MY STATE,
MY NATION!"

It must begin, though, with self—lest ye know not
the hour nor the day that He has turned His back on
thee.   3976-25

Is not that promise of prayer power as valid today as it
was in 1940?

PSYCHOANALYSIS AND THE EDGAR CAYCE
READINGS

Dudley Delany

Introduction

It is a commonly held belief among the spiritually minded
that—with its thoroughly materialistic *Weltanschauung*
and its heavy emphasis upon sexual determinants—nothing
good can come out of psychoanalysis. Hence it is seldom a
topic of conversation among such individuals, and its
founder, Sigmund Freud, is generally regarded by them as
persona non grata. However, once we are quite sure of
what, why, and in whom we believe, the examination and
evaluation of psychoanalysis ceases to be a threatening experience and becomes, rather, an enlightening one. For
psychoanalysis deals not only with theory, however bizarre
it may at times appear, but also with fact—the fact of
human behavior and experience, which psychoanalysis is in
a uniquely favorable position to observe. To ignore the
facts presented by this discipline is to do an injustice both
to it and to oneself.

Our concern in the present paper is to bring
together—admittedly, but necessarily, in the most pre-

liminary manner—the facts of psychoanalytic observation and the statements (we assume them to be facts) contained in the readings of Edgar Cayce. We are here dealing essentially with two universes of discourse, and we want to ascertain at what points, if any, they intersect. We are thus looking for relationships between the two, with the hope that a new and greater understanding will come about of them and of ourselves. Let us begin, then, with a key concept—one which psychoanalysts consider to be the nucleu of most, if not all, neurotic conflict: the *Oedipus complex*.

The Oedipus Complex

The situation in which the child craves the exclusive possession of the parent of the opposite sex, and simultaneously feels hostility toward and desire to remove the parent of the same sex, is called the Oedipus complex. The existence of the Oedipus complex is daily confirmed in the analytic situation, and even non-analytically trained observers witness its expression in the commonly voiced desire on the part of a young child to marry Mommy (in the case of the boy) or Daddy (in the case of the girl). Obviously, such a possessive craving, which usually contains powerful erotic overtones, is doomed to go unfulfilled, and, because of its unacceptable nature, is almost sure to be forcibly removed from consciousness (repressed).

The handling of the Oedipus complex is seen as being an important factor in one's adjustment to people and situations in later life. But what, you may ask, has all this to do with the Cayce readings? Just this; the readings teach us to recognize the possibility—indeed, the high probability—that our children are not, after all, strangers to us, that we and they have known one another in former experiences, and that we have most likely been through much together. On many occasions, readings were given which depicted very strong bonds between family members, which were based not so much on the present life and its happenings as on former incarnations. Thus it is not incredible to expect a man's wife in this life to incarnate as his daughter in his next experience; in which case,

51

therefore, is it any wonder that the little girl, at some level of her personality, feels jealous and hostile towards her mother, desires to possess her father exclusively, and craves him as an object of love, companionship, and sexual gratification? The riddle of the Oedipus complex becomes clear in the light of reincarnation, and seems far more intelligible than the analytic assumption that the little girl's craving and desire for her father are based largely upon the fact that he possesses an organ which she does not, and that she feels antagonism towards her mother for having failed to provide her with one. We do not wholly dismiss the analytic assumption; we merely put it in proper perspective.

In the same vein, it is not too much to expect that mother's little helper was her passionate lover in a previous incarnation and that the little boy now harbors forbidden feelings towards her of a most positive nature, as well as a good measure of negative feelings towards his father. Here the analytic assumption is more palatable, for it envisions such mixed emotions as arising naturally out of the boy's long period of dependence upon his mother and out of the necessity of sharing her love and attention with his father.

Of course, no two parent-child relationships are the same, so a child need not enter the present experience with anything like the kind of background we have just considered. To be sure, psychoanalysis has recognized the fact that the Oedipus complex is very strong in some and that in others it is very weak. Under the reincarnation hypothesis such variability is to be expected, since not every little boy was once his mother's lover, and so forth. Even Freud could not explain the vagaries of the Oedipus complex solely in terms of the experiences of the present incarnation. He thus found it necessary, in his *Outline of Psychoanalysis,* to fall back on an *archaic heredity,* the notion of racial memories which result from the experiences of our ancestors, which form part of our unconscious, and which, therefore, influence our present reactions and behavior. We must admit that Freud was not far wrong. He failed to see only that *we* are our ancestors.

The readings imply that one of the functions of the

Oedipus situation is to thwart personal love, with its exclusiveness and possessiveness, and to leave in its place the same impersonal, all-embracing love expressed by Jesus, toward the development of which we are all heading. Thus the Oedipus complex plays an important part in spiritual evolution.

If anything, the readings put the psychoanalytically derived concept of the Oedipus complex on a firmer foundation than it otherwise could ever have hoped for.

The Psychology of Religion

As we all know, psychoanalysis disavows religion, relegates it to the status of an illusion, and deems it the product of wishful thinking. The only purpose religion serves is to give man a false sense of security, we are told. Now, whatever we may think of this position, certain facts turn up in analytic investigation which point strongly to the existence of some kind of relationship between religion and the family constellation and, in particular, our relationship with our father. Thus it may be very difficult for a man to turn towards God if he is dominated by an unconscious death wish directed towards his father. At any rate, the readings state that the family represents the pattern of man's relationship to God (an idea which is in keeping, of course, with the general rule that the material is a reflection of the spiritual). It is an enormously complex relationship, and the present writer cannot begin to untangle it here. Still, it seems clear enough that what Freud has done is to take the fact of this relationship and transform it into a *cause,* and by doing so violates one of the major tenets of science. Science never assumes that if A is correlated with B, then A causes B or B causes A, since there is always the possibility that a third variable, C, is intervening to cause both A and B.

Anxiety

Psychoanalysis sees birth—the separation of the infant from its cozy relationship to its mother—as the prototype of all later anxiety reactions. The Cayce readings, on the other hand, view man's initial separation from God as the

53

point at which anxiety first made its appearance. By implication, the closer we come to our original relationship with God, the less becomes the press of anxiety. It is not a matter of wonder, therefore, that religion acts to allay anxiety and to buttress man against environmental stress.

Meditation and Therapy

In his *New Introductory Lectures on Psychoanalysis,* Freud expresses the conviction that "certain practices of mystics" (we assume that he was referring to meditation and similar measures) bear a relation to psychoanalysis in that they, too, serve to widen one's field of vision, and to extend consciousness downward to include hitherto unconquered portions of the unconscious. He did not believe, however, that such practices could put one in possession of "ultimate truths," from which all good would flow; and in this he deviates sharply from the position of the Cayce readings, which view meditation as the *sine qua non* of spiritual growth.

Of course, Freud conceived of the unconscious as little more than a seething cauldron of primitive drives and urges. He did not seem to realize that it contains not only the very worst, but also the very best in man. So the psychoanalyst holds that there is nothing that meditation can do which psychoanalysis cannot do better; while the spiritual minded contend that there is nothing psychoanalysis can do which meditation cannot do better. Actually, it would seem that neither position is tenable, and that there is a place for both in the general scheme of things. For while both procedures aim to expand consciousness, they differ radically in the *direction* of this expansion. Psychoanalysis expands consciousness in the direction of repressed drives, forbidden wishes, conflict, and frustration. This is done with the hope, for which there is ample justification (for no well-informed individual doubts that psychoanalytic psychotherapy gets results), that the conscious personality will thereby gain mastery and control over these disturbing phenomena.

Meditation, by contrast, expands consciousness in the direction of the *Divine* within, with the hope, for which there is also ample justification, that the God force will take hold upon the personality and exert a constructive, guiding, and healing influence. Meditation bypasses the conflict areas and goes straight to the very source of life, the indwelling spirit of God. Meditation does not aim for conflict resolution, as does psychoanalysis. How, then, are its benefits similar to those of analysis? The answer to this question lies in the fact that it is not conflict, *per se,* which does the mischief, but the *place* which the conflict occupies in our psychic structure.

Meditation, besides being a healing agent in its own right, thus brings about a change in the distribution of psychic energy, such that our conflicts and frustrations cease to be troublesome and disappear in *effect,* if not in actuality. They lose their importance, their demand quality, their energic dominance, if you will, in the economy of our mental apparatus (or mental body, as Cayce would say). What this means is that those who have learned to meditate effectively are indeed fortunate. It means that meditation should be a part of every measure to come to grips with emotional problems, from the standpoint of both treatment and prevention. It also means that when meditation is disturbed by external or internal stress, the old conflicts will come back, perhaps more forcefully than before, although we would expect that in time the cumulative effect of meditation would be to destroy altogether their influence as part of its healing effect.

But what about the person (such as the severely neurotic and psychotic, or normal but unusually harried individual) who is too disturbed to sit down and meditate or to achieve the level of meditation requisite for healing and for the redistribution of psychic energy? There can be no doubt that once fears, doubts, complexes, guilt feelings, and other negative emotions and attitudes are purged by psychoanalytic treatment, an individual is much better fitted to enter into the holy sanctuary of the body and to attain a mature and stable relationship to the Divine within.

We know from our work with the Cayce readings that osteopathy can also effect a redistribution and, in psychotic states, a complete reorganization of forces in the mental apparatus. The implications of this fact should be of untold significance for psychoanalytic, psychological, and psychiatric theory, practice, and research.

Dreams

No discussion of either Cayce or psychoanalysis would be complete without a word about dreams.

The reader will recall that it was Freud who made the statement that "dreams are the royal road to the unconscious." Indeed, it is largely due to the influence of psychoanalysis that the study of dreams is given any credence in contemporary thought.

To be sure, Freud's view of the dream was rather limited, since for him every dream was only a wish fulfillment. The Cayce readings, on the other hand, give one the impression that there is practically nothing that a dream cannot and does not in some way express, including glimpses of the future and of the archaic past.

In dreams, too, Freud recognized the influence of memories and experiences that could not have been acquired in one given lifetime. He was also aware that some dreams contain evidences of psychical phenomena such as telepathy. With regard to Freud's observations of these and other phenomena, he once stated in a letter to a friend, "If I had my life to live over again, I should devote myself to psychical research rather than to psychoanalysis." This wish may well come true, for Freud will most assuredly have his life to live over again, at which time we may witness the development of a new, enlightened, and Christian psychoanalysis. With the help of such spiritual springs as the Cayce readings, this may come about even in our own time, without Freud's material participation.

Conclusion

Although we have by no means exhausted this subject matter, it is already apparent that there is everything to gain and nothing to lose from a critical appraisal of the relationship between psychoanalysis and the Cayce readings. For truth abides in both, and it is to truth that we should ever turn.

HEALTH IN YOUR LIFE DESIGN

Roy D. Kirkland, D.O.

The triune of body-mind-soul cannot be separated in the consideration of health on the highest plane. Is not agony of soul reflected in bodily function? Can mental activity be separated from the body pattern?

Today there are indications that we are beginning to face more clearly the health challenge in respect to the whole man—his body-mind-soul relationship—rather than viewing his condition from the purely symptomatic approach. Consequently, when we approach the subject of health in life design, whether achieving it, maintaining it, or recovering it, we are interested in three phases: the *pre-natal, post-natal,* and *post-mortal.* And for a proper perspective on one's own health, the following divisions of influence may be considered:

> *Mind, the Builder*
> *Environment, the Workshop*
> *Emotion, the Conditioner*

Mind, the Builder

If one had all the references that Edgar Cayce made to mind function on strips of paper like those used in the A.R.E. Library, he could make a paper chain, no doubt, that would reach to Telstar with a few cosmic streamers left over. And, if he added to this all the invitations to elaboration that these references impose on the thinking, searching individual, he might come up with a chain that would reach to the original Edgar Cayce reference shelf in some inter-galactic library! Through all of these runs the simple basic statement that *Mind is the Builder.*

"Every thought is followed by a physical reaction of some

57

kind," is the way William James, the great Harvard psychologist, put it. In fewer words and more graphically, Edgar Cayce said:

That as MIND dwells upon is BUILDED. 257-53

In a reading Mr. Cayce gave to a middle-aged woman who asked, "Is there likelihood of bad health in March?" he answered:

If you're looking for it, you can have it in February! If you would skip March, skip it—you'll have it in June. If you want to skip June, don't have it at all this year.   3564

He went on, however, to advise the woman quite specifically in matters of diet and later had a letter from her in which she stated. "God is wonderfully blessing you, and through you blessing the world."

When we accept that Mind *Is* the Builder, and realize fully that thought is preface to action, and the sum total of our life accomplishment can be computed by the thought forms imaged within the mind, then we can see the importance of being on guard at the gates of our senses—directing thought that stems from these senses so that the resultant reactions will be in line with our highest ideals and goals.

We hear so much of automation in our time—of programming this or that type of computer. Let us hear much more of programming the God-given mechanism within us, processing it with good thoughts and high ideals in an orderly fashion—ORDER being one of the original laws of godly creation and success. If we program our minds with attitudes of *friendly approach, objectivity, unselfishness, humor* and *attention* (*attention* as opposed to indifference or mental lethargy that make us vulnerable to the hard-sell and subliminal techniques of this age)—if we program our minds with *purpose* that is worthy, idealistic, practical, unbiased, cosmic—if we make *order, patience,* and *balance* dominant postures in the overall program of thought direction—and we train ourselves to be aware of the rhythms of life (biological, global, cosmic)—then what place is there for the destructive, the negative, the retrogressive that is seedbed for the various pathogens that confront man as ailments?

I would like to present to you at this point *An Ancient Formula for Repelling Disease:*

I *Three Drops of Pity,* a steady flow of compassion, and the gastric juices shall go about their work uninterrupted, and there shall be no stones nor inflamation.

II *Three Ounces of Unselfishness,* generosity of thought and deed, and the body shall not be a prey to fevers, sending its warmth outward.

III *Seven Lungfuls of Laughter and Lovelit Speech,* a habitual outpouring of joy, and the throat cannot ache and swell in its longing for laughter, and the tongue cannot parch in the absence of healing, medicinal words.

IV *Four Tumblers of Charity,* a soothing and inexpensive cordial, and the very bones of us will respond, every joint and sinew laved and oiled by its grace.

V *One Injection of Far Memory,* suffused through every vein, and the heart shall beat in harmony with the systole and diastole of life design.

VI *Two Swallows of Patience,* nature's favorite remedy, and the eyes shall not lose their power of sight and insight.

VII *A Long Steady Diet of Silence and Inner Control,* the ancient hospital bed, and the brain shall not waver nor short circuit, keeping her metered pace.

VIII *Five Tablets from the Mills of Conscience,* however bitter to the taste, and the ears cannot shut to the cries of heaven in the dust frames about us.

IX *Six Transfusions of Prayer on a Scale as Grand as the Cosmos,* a remedy the most indigent may grasp, and the rich blood and the complex cell may not be attacked nor disordered.*

* From ON THE TRELLIS OF MEMORY, an unpublished work by Elithe Hamilton Kirkland and Jenny Lind Porter

All who have given as much as a skimming glance at the topical index on the Cayce readings will recall the abundance of the references to the mind functions set forth in this formula as significant in repelling disease—to mention only a few: *Compassion . . . Joy . . . Unselfishness . . . Patience . . . Prayer.*

"Be oft in prayer," Cayce said over and over. "Be glad! . . . Be joyous! . . . Cultivate laughter . . . Appreciate wit and humor."

The author of these nine activities for repelling disease might have been at least a soul comrade to Edgar Cayce, for certainly he, too, knew MIND as the BUILDER.

Environment, the Workshop

Environment is quite literally the workshop of both mind and body, offering many stimuli in the execution of one's life design. It may also offer one suggestions of what he did with environment in past experiences, what he should be doing now, and what environmental consequences may be projected post-mortally—that is, into future earth experiences.

In one of his early readings, given almost forty years ago for a young student of philosophy, Mr. Cayce carried on a lively discussion about heredity and environment. He mentioned a scientific study that had set forth certain environmental conditions as being the cause of insanity (Brennan's study of 20,000 cases—Reading 900-34). Mr. Cayce noted that such studies had gone on for ages and would go on for ages to come trying to determine whether heredity or environment has the greater part in one's development. The answer, he said is "the application of will in either direction."

Has the entity in its experience through its will applied that of will toward the development . . .

(He's speaking of development through various earth experiences—)

. . . or has it allowed ITSELF TO BE USED by the environment and become subject to environment;

or, has it developed itself through its will toward its own hereditary position—for all the children of God. How has the development led?

This would imply that if we have been "used by the environment" in previous life experiences so that we find ourselves here and now surrounded by the unhealthful, the unbeautiful, the disorderly, then *will (thought direction)* must come into play to affect changes, else we will find ourselves on reentry in similiar adverse environment. The good diet, the proper exercise and recreation, the pure water and air, the harmonies of nature, of color and sound, may not be set before us again to invite our inattentiveness and preoccupation with superficial and purposeless pursuits.

Strong environmental stimuli for healthful development of body-mind-soul are in the natural forces around you: the *ground* you are rooted in . . . the *land* you tread upon . . . the *air* you breathe . . . the *waters* you drink and delight in . . . the *vegetation* you see and commune with and use in your diet (the very *light* that affects this vegetation—its blossoming and harvest and biochemical synthesis). These are standard equipment in your workshop, whether scanty or bountiful, whether polluted, depleted, or vital with natural energy.

Sounds . . . Shapes . . . Colors . . . Scents . . . Rhythms . . . These five agents constantly engulf you and solicit your responses, consciously or unconsciously. Your workshop is literally thundering and throbbing with *rhythms:* your habit rhythms . . . your biological and psychological rhythms . . . mechanical and nature rhythms . . . people rhythms and global rhythms . . . rhythms of the earth, its winds and waters and other functions as wondrous and complex as those of the human body . . . rhythms planetary and cosmic that we can intuit if not encompass with our calendars and consciousness . . . and the constant rhythms of *sound,* both harmonious and destructive.

In the area of *sound,* there is one province where the individual has very personal direction over the effects. That is in the use of the WORD—the vibrations coming from both the tonal structure of the word and the nuances given to it by the mind and voice of the speaker. The environmental stimuli of communication are vital forces in one's development. When damage is done by word, the greater negative result is on the user. The *echoic backlash of tonal thrust* (the actual sound vibration) from an oath of imprecation is on the one who utters it. We are now in an age of sonics—growing application of sound vibrations in medicine, both diagnostically and therapeutically, in space science, and other fields. Even the atom has its tone—its melody.

Edgar Cayce referred often to the vibrations of *sound and color* as being influential in the individual's mental and physical growth and state of health. We see very elaborate uses of both forces as major props and devices in merchandising and entertainment. And how well we know that if the gates of our senses are left wide open and unguarded, we are eating, drinking, seeing, thinking, buying and performing in puppet fashion, caught up in the fingerplay of color and sound stimuli.

There is a world of music, a world of beauty in color that can stimulate us to perform for our higher selves, creating and using environment instead of being used by it. The element of beauty in environment and person makes life more spectacular, more abundant, and more replete with the energies that build health and happiness into the life design.

Diet, exercise, and recreation are essential equipment in the environmental workshop of Mind, the Builder. Our health authorities supply us bountifully with literature and instruction in these fields, but there is a special need in these times to think of foods as more than items on a diet list or as stimuli to taste buds and salivary glands. We need to consider where food is grown, the soil nutrients . . . how it is grown (naturally or under heavy hurry-hurry chemical fertilization that increases sugar and decreases proteins, and with fleet applications of insecticides) . . . how it is processed (has life been destroyed and lifeless substitute been added?). The organic farmer will more and more fill our needs as time goes on. Mr. Cayce advised the importance of having soil of our own in times ahead for just such production. We have desensitized, defoliated, debacterialized, DESTROYED many of the life-giving organic elements in order to produce great

62

mountains of lifeless food. Certainly the attitude and will can assist the marvelous mechanisms of adjustment and adaptation in the human body to make the most of the little substance in some of these foods. But the body structure, the temple, needs some strong beams, some good foundations and guarded doors. More and more we are going to have to provide these by our own efforts or by cooperative effort.

At the same time, we must give attention to the air and water that sustain both ourselves and the vegetation we are dependent upon. We know the serious concern now being given air and water pollution. The scientists and other authorities tell us that if this pollution continues at the present rate, by the year 2000 all vegetation will be killed.

In our health considerations we are becoming more aware of the stimuli from magnetic fields such as the north and south poles, the electro-magnetic fields, and even the positive and negative poles in the body which affect the acid-alkaline balance of the body. In some recent experimental work, it was learned that the electro-magnetic fields in office buildings were such as to affect the efficiency and thinking capabilities of those working in the area. The higher the floor from the ground, the greater the loss in efficiency. The capability index of the worker was in proportion to the strength of the field—the distance from the ground to the floor the worker might be on, and the voltage in the wiring system—whether the wires were parallel or criss-crossed or some other design creating the field.

Our *wills* and our *attentions* have big business on hand relative to the conditions prevailing in our workshops, both personal and global—much to handle effectively with *thought direction* (individually and in groups), much to govern through power of *will*, if we are to claim health.

Emotion, the Conditioner

In one of the many Cayce statements on emotions, particular attention was given the glandular system:

The emotions act as the pulsators of glandular

63

function, giving the impulse to the nerve centers, and thus the function will vary according to the type of emotion or origin of the impulse.   294

In practical application, this would mean that the function of the Builder would vary according to the origin of the impulse.

I would emphasize the importance of the happy mood, the joyful expressions, thoughtfulness of self and all others because these emotions condition the type of thinking affecting the thyroid and adrenal glands especially. As for the negative effects:

> You can take a bad cold from getting mad. You you can take a bad cold from blessing [cursing] out someone else, even if it's your wife!   849-75

Kindness and other constructive attitudes which stimulate the mechanisms of happiness, contentment, and creativity within us, in turn give constructive stimuli to the various systems of the body: the glandular, the digestive, the cardio-vascular, and the eliminative systems including intestinal, genito-urinary, perspiratory, respiratory, etc.

On the other hand, the negative vibrations—the emotions of jealousy, envy, disappointment, frustration, fear, and hate, and the multiple gradations of selfishness might well be the forerunners or contributing factors in such abnormalities as asthma and heart conditions, cancer and diabetes, as well as other ailments.

These influences of positive and negative vibrations, the conditioners which Mind, the Builder, is subject unto, affect to some degree the bio-chemistry and bio-physics of every cell, every organ, and every group of organs making up the total body functions. Thus we can calculate the importance of directing our thoughts to govern our emotions so that we may have the health of body and mind to claim that which we desire in life—that most vital to our souls' development—so that we make the best use of past experiences and project the best of which we are now capable into the next stage of our terrestial journey.

All bodies are amenable to suggestion," Edgar Cayce stated in reading for 4648, "through the abnormal mind, or through the subconscious mind, or through the sympathetic nervous system of the body."

The body is capable of thinking of only one thing at a time; consequently, if it is kept busy thinking of the right things, there is no place for negative thought—no unguarded post at which suggestions of violence and hatred or the hard sell can make passage.

And now, we might ask, what has all this to do with HEALTH from *pre-natal* and *post-mortal* viewpoints? Since the physical and mental development (and, analytically, the soul development) depend upon the strength and character of the formative vibrations, it is evident that what we think and act upon—what we project—is greatly influenced by the health pattern. And so, the unfolding of the projected nucleus or energy into the following incarnation will carry that which we have builded in this life, along with the accumulation of past lives. A Cayce reading put this very directly:

3517-2 Q-3 *"Please give origin of all the trouble."*
(Referring to coccyx difficulty.)
A-3 "It began 25,000 years ago! This is the trouble."

and again in 3504-1 . . .

Sources of these disturbances are prenatal as well as karmic. These, of course, may be rejected by many. Yet these who rejected same do not supply better reasons, do they?

A mother, upon early consultation with a physician following conception, is advised as to diet, supplement, mood, and exercise—and by some is further instructed as to mental attitudes for proper approach to pregnancy, purposeful desires, and suitable projections for the offspring. These are important, but even before this the contemplating parents should consider the purpose of conception and the high ideal surrounding conception for the purpose of preparing the fertile seedbed as a suitable environment for soul entrance and development. In addition to this, there are the forces, as Mr. Cayce brought forward, that project embryonic implantation as related to karmic need and soul evolution (2175-8), He informed an entity that the decision he thought was made on January 1, 1944, was really made first in the month of December in the year 1020—nine hundred and twenty-four years before.

During our sojourn in the earth plane, we are faced constantly with the positive or negative choices and influences, and with body responses to the magnetic fields. This is man's challenge: to understand and achieve *balance*—to find a median between these forces, not swaying too far to the right or the left, setting his path on the straight and narrow Way. Instruction in *balance* could be one of the big reasons why we come into this plane of existence. The great Paramahansa Yogananda, whose thinking and works have given much worthy instruction for our time, said that the material and the spiritual are two parts of one universe and one truth. Yogananda cautioned that emphasis on one or the other retarded man's development of balance. He asserted that properly guided thoughts, desires and actions would lead to a higher state of consciousness.

No better emphasis could be given this statement on balance than another quotation from the Edgar Cayce records:

> Each soul is a temple of the living God. Thus be more mindful of the body, not for the body's sake, that it may be a better channel for manifesting spiritual truths. 2938-1

So, let us program the mind and direct our thoughts through the will to unite with the opportunities of the spiritual forces, that man may come from the darkness of dis-ease and anxieties into the light and freedom of the cosmic intent.

THE PURPOSE FOR REINCARNATION

from the Edgar Cayce Readings

The life readings given by the late Edgar Cayce are obviously based on the assumption that the theory of rebirth is not theory, but fact. They describe in some detail past lives in the earth, and the problems or abilities resulting from those lives. They were given to the individuals to explain and to help them in their present lives. The reading given for 798-4 explains the reason why souls reincarnate.

Hence when the entity enters the earth plane (with which we are dealing in the present, and which is to be used for each opportunity that is presented for an activity of the mental and soul forces) it is but a period again and again of the application either of the universal forces, that make for a oneness of activity of the soul; or an activity in what becomes the fruitage thereof as destructive forces, or hardships, or influences that make for tempering of the soul for its purposes, its activities, its desires throughout an experience.   798-4

Many people when coming upon the concept of reincarnation for the first time prefer to examine the idea in the light of what is taught in the orthodox churches and in the Bible. The same questions are put to the Edgar Cayce readings. In the following extract we find not only an explanation for the reincarnation of souls in the earth, but we note that much of the explanation is a paraphrase of the Gospel according to St. John. Here, then, is the direct tie-in of reincarnation with Christianity, with the demonstration that a belief in each does not deny, but supplements the other.

Q-8. What is the lesson that may be drawn from my entrance into the present plane?
A-8. That purpose for which the soul entered in, under those circumstances and conditions in the earth's experience in the present, that the soul might meet in this experience that which will make for the more sureness in Him. For, the earth is His and the fulness thereof. For, as given, God and the Christ Spirit is Life itself; and the motivating force of the soul is either for that companionship, that association, that development which will make such a soul-body as a fit companion for that Creative Influence manifested in the earth in Him, or it is for separating self from Him. For, in the Beginning was

the Word, and that Spirit, that Christ Spirit *was* the Word. That Word was made flesh, even as each soul that manifests in the earth is made flesh. That soul, that spirit, *dwelt* among men, and that soul made itself of no estate; yet the Creator, the Maker, the Giver of the life itself; that man, that each soul, that his soul, might know that it has an advocate *with* the Father through Him that gave Himself as a ransom. How? For, as the impulses in self arise, know those impulses have arisen in Him; yet through the ability to overcome death in the material world is His presence able to abide with thee, dost thou trust in Him and not in self. Or, as He gave, in Him who *is* the Maker and the Creator is life alone, and they that put their trust in anything else climb up some other way. But they that put their trust in Him are His, and He calleth them by name, and He abideth with them. When ye call on Him He is very near.

Know, then, that in this experience thou mayest come to know Him as thine daily companion in whatsoever thou doest; for, "If ye love me, keep my commandments." What are His commandments? A new commandment He gave, that ye love one another, even as He hast loved thee.   524-2

THE ESSENES AND MOUNT CARMEL

Violet M. Shelley

As early as 1936 the Edgar Cayce readings had been alluding to a community of Essenes who once lived on Mount Carmel, describing in detail past lives in that community, as well as its religious practices, ideals and purposes. Stating that *Essenes* meant "expectancy," the information that came through the clairvoyance of Cayce asserted that the group stemmed from the school of prophets which was established in Elijah's time, and was dedicated to preparing a channel for the coming of the Messiah. Familiarity with this esoteric brotherhood could not be laid to Cayce's knowledge of the Scriptures, since the Essenes are not mentioned in the Bible. Neither can such profusion of intimate detail be ascribed to an interest in the Dead Sea Scrolls, for when the attention of the world was drawn to the Essenes by the discovery of the scrolls, that attention was focused on Qumran, not on Mount Carmel, and Edgar Cayce was no longer living.

Thirty years after the first mention of Mount Carmel and the Essenes, an investigative group traveled to the area in search of clues that might point toward eventual proof. The readings had said that the present day order of Carmelites had their origin in that Essene community, yet available reference material traces the origin only to the Crusades. In interviews with a Father Elias at Stella Maris Monastery, the group was surprised to learn that present-day Carmelites live with a wealth of legend and tradition that traces their way of life to Elijah, and a band of long forgotten Jewish monks. While Father Elias was careful to point out that many traditions are based on piety rather than historical fact, he also pointed out that particularly in that part of the world legends often contain a germ of truth. Although there is no recognized connection between the Carmelites and the Essenes as such, Father Elias did admit that the Essenes were the only known Jewish group at the time of Jesus who could be said to resemble a monastic order. The Essenes, he said, were true monks, since monks are made by their vows.

As Mount Carmel has barely been touched archeologically, it is quite possible that evidence of the Essene community mentioned in the Cayce records may one day be found.

From the Edgar Cayce Readings

For the entity Eloise then was in that capacity as one of the holy women who ministered in the temple service and in the preparation of those who dedicated their lives for individual activity during that sojourn.

The entity was then what would be termed in the

present in some organizations as a Sister Superior, as an officer, as it were, in those of the Essenes and their preparation.

Hence we find the entity, then, giving, giving, ministering, encouraging, making for the greater activities; and making for those encouraging experiences oft in the lives of the Disciples; coming in contact with the Master oft in the ways between Bethany, Galilee, Jerusalem. For, as indicated, the entity kept the school on the way above Emmaus to the way that "goeth down toward Jericho" and towards the northernmost coast from Jerusalem. The entity blessed many of those who came to seek to know the teachings, the ways, the mysteries, the understandings; for the entity had been trained in the schools of those that were of the prophets and prophetesses, and the entity was indeed a prophetess in those experiences—thus gained throughout.

(1391-1; June 22, 1937)

The entity was closely associated with the priests who were active in the Carmelian area, where there had been the early teachings established years ago by Elijah, Elisha, Samuel; that taught the mysteries of man and his relationships to those forces as might manifest from within and without.

(2520-1; June 23, 1941)

In those days when there had been more and more of the leaders of the people in Carmel—the original place where the school of prophets was established during Elijah's time, Samuel—these were called then Essenes: and those that were students of what ye would call astrology, numerology, phrenology, and those phases of that study of the return of individuals—or incarnation. (5749-8; June 27, 1937)

When there first began those of John's (Baptist) teachings we find the entity then joined rather those of the Essene group. For John (Baptist) first taught that women who chose might dedicate their lives to a specific service. Hence, not only the brothers, but

70

those employed by the brothers, Peter, Andrew, Judas (not Iscariot) joined in the activities.

(540-4; February 20, 1936)

For Zebedee first was a follower of John, then of those that separated themselves from the Jewish Sanhedrin, the Jewish Law, and of the head of the Essenes in those studies to which both John the Baptist and the Master came first as teacher, and as instructors.   (1089-3; January 23, 1936)

With the establishing of the church of Jerusalem, the entity was present when James . . . the brother of the Lord . . . was raised to that position or place as the head of the church, through the direct influence of James and John the sons of Zebedee. This brought about that first of the authorities putting forth their hand and slaying James by the sword. This happened not by that of trial, but by that as would today be called a riot; and not incorrectly were James and John called the sons of thunder.

(2390-3; March 8, 1941)

There the entity was as the COMPANION of the scribe, Ezra; making those activities which brought into the experiences of the young what might be called the reestablishing of the school that had been a part of Elijah's experience in Mt. Carmel.

(2444-1; February 4, 1941)

The entity was among those who were students of the law, those who were interested in the activities having to do with questionings pertaining to the law that had been interpreted from the priests and rabbis of the day pertaining to the Mosaic law, and the interesting facts and fancies that had come from the eastern lands, from which the Wise Men had come. These, as parts of the teachings, had become adopted by those groups of the Essenes of which John and Joseph and Mary had been a part before the entering of the Master, Jesus in the earth.

(3344-2; March 29, 1944)

71

. . . In giving the biographical life of the entity Josie, much of those activities might be indicated that brought about those later relationships with Mary, the mother of Jesus.

As has been outlined from here, there were those special groups of individuals who had made some preparations for the expected activities that were to come about during that particular period; especially those of the Essenes who had chosen the twelve maidens to indicate their fitness. This choice was to be made by those selections indicated by the spirit, and Josie was the daughter of Shem and Mephibosheth that was among those.

This entity, Josie, was close to Mary when the selection was indicated by the shadow or the angel on the stair, at that period of consecration in the temple. This was not the temple in Jerusalem, but the temple where those who were consecrated worshiped, or a school—as it might be termed—for those who might be channels.

This was a part of that group of Essenes who, headed by Judy, made those interpretations of those activities from the Egyptian experience,—as the Temple Beautiful, and the service in the Temple of Sacrifice. Hence it was in this consecrated place where this selection took place.

Then, when there was the fulfilling of those periods when Mary was espoused to Joseph and was to give birth to the Savior, the Messiah, the Prince of Peace, the Way, the Truth, the Light,—soon after this birth there was the issuing of the orders first by Judy that there should be someone selected to be with the parents during their period of sojourn in Egypt. This was owing to the conditions which arose from the visit of the Wise Men and their not returning to Herod to report, when the decrees were issued that there should be the destruction of the children of that age from six months to two years, especially in that region from Bethany to Nazareth.

Thus this entity, Josie, was selected or chosen by those of the Brotherhood—sometimes called White

Brotherhood in the present—as the handmaid or companion of Mary, Jesus and Joseph, in their flight into Egypt.

This began on an evening, and the journey—through portions of Palestine, from Nazareth to the borders of Egypt—was made only during the night.

Do not understand that there was only Joseph, Mary, Josie and the Child. For there were other groups that preceded and followed; that there might be the physical protection to that as had been considered by these groups of peoples as the fulfilling of the Promised One.

In the journey to Egypt, little of great significance might be indicated, but the care and attention to the Child and the Mother was greatly in the hands of this entity, Josie, through that journey.

The period of sojourn in Egypt was in and about, or close to, what was then Alexandria.

Josie and Mary were not idle during that period of sojourn, but those records—that had been a part of those activities preserved in portions of the libraries there—were a part of the work that had been designated for this entity. And the interest in same was reported to the Brotherhood in the Judean country.

The sojourn there was a period of some four years—four years, six months, three days.

When there were those beginnings of the journey back to the Promised Land, there were naturally—from some of the records that had been read by the entity Josie, as well as the parents—the desires to know whether there were those unusual powers indicated in this child now, that was in every manner a normal, developed body, ready for those activities of children of that particular period.

But do not interpret same in the light of childhood in thine own land in the present—more in the light of the oriental. For, remember, in Egypt as well as parts of Galilee were the customs and activities of those to whom the care of this physical entity was entrusted through that early sojourn in the earth.

73

The return was made to Capernaum—not Nazareth—not only for political reasons owing to the death of Herod but the division that had been made with the kingdom after the death of Herod; and that there might be the ministry or teaching that was to be a part of the Brotherhood,—supervised in that period by Judy, as among the leaders of the Essenes in that particular period.

Hence much of the early education, the early activities, were those prompted or directed by that leader in that particular experience, but were administered by—or in the closer associations by—Josie. Though from the idea of the Brotherhood the activities of the entity were no longer necessitated, the entity Josie preferred to remain—and did remain until those periods when there was the sending or the administering of the teachings to the young Master, first in Persia and later in India, and then in Egypt again—where there were the completions.

But the entity, Josie, following the return, was active in all the educational activities as well as in the care of the body and the attending to those things pertaining to the household duties with every developing child. And Josie was among those who went with Mary and Joseph when they went to the city, or to Jerusalem, at the time of the age of twelve. It was thought by Joseph and Mary that it was in the care of Josie that He had stayed, when He was missed, in those periods when there was the returning to find Him in the temple.

Josie was with Mary throughout those activities. And is it any wonder that when there were those preparations of the body for burial that Josie was the one who brought the spices, the ointments that were to consecrate the preparations of this body for whom it had cared through those early periods of its experience in the earth?

Through that period Josie never married, and was known among the Holy Women throughout the period; coming and persuading the Mother, Mary, when there was the arrest, to come to Jerusalem.

The entity passed on through those periods of

riots following the beheading of James, the brother of John.

Ready for questions.

Q-1. What association with the entity who is now (294) did I have in the Palestine experience?

A-1.   The teacher of the Master knew only of Lucius through those activities in Laodicea,—for he came at the time of Pentecost, see?

Q-2.   What was the nature of the records studied by Josie in Egypt?

A-2.   Those same records from which the men of the East said and gave, "By those records we have seen his star." These pertained, then, to what you would call today astrological forecasts, as well as those records which had been compiled and gathered by all of those of that period pertaining to the coming of the Messiah. These had been part of the records from those in Carmel, in the early experiences, as of those given by Elijah,—who was the forerunner, who was the cousin, who was the Baptist. All of these had been a part of the records—pertaining not only to the nature of work of the parents but as to their places of sojourn, and the very characteristics that would indicate these individuals; the nature and the character that would be a part of the experiences to those coming in contact with the young Child; as to how the garments worn by the Child would heal children. For the body being perfect radiated that which was health, life itself. Just as today, individuals may radiate, by their spiritual selves, health, life, that vibration which is destruction to dis-ease in any form in bodies. These were the characters and natures of things studied by Josie.

For, is it not quoted oft, "All of these things she kept and pondered them in her heart"? With what? With the records that Josie as well as herself had seen. These records were destroyed, of course, in a much later period.

Q-3.   Can any more details be given as to the training of the child?

A-3.   Only those that covered the period from six years to about sixteen, which were in keeping with the tenets of the Brotherhood; as well as that training in the law,—which was the Jewish or Mosaic law in that period. This was read, this was interpreted in accordance with those activities defined and outlined for the parents and the companions of the developing body. Remember and keep in mind, He was normal, He developed normally. Those about Him saw those characteristics that may be anyone's who wholly puts the trust in God! And to every parent might it not be said, daily, dedicate thy life that thy offspring may be called of God into service—to the glory of God and to the honor of thy name!

(1010-17; June 21, 1942)

... Here we may give even portions of the records as scribed by the entity called Judy, as the teacher, as the healer, as the prophetess through that experience.

Some four and twenty years before the advent of that entity, that soul-entrance into material plane called Jesus, we find Phinehas (?) and Elkatma (?) making those activities among those of the depleted group of the prophets in Mt. Carmel; that begun by Samuel, Elisha, Elijah, Saul, and those during those early experiences.

Because of the divisions that had arisen among the peoples into sects, as the Pharisee, the Sadducee and their divisions, there had arisen the Essenes that had cherished not merely the conditions that had come as word of mouth but had kept the records of the periods when individuals had been visited with the supernatural or out of the ordinary experiences; whether in dreams, visions, voices, or what not that had been and were felt by these students of the customs, of the law, of the activities throughout the experiences of this peculiar people—the promises and the many ways these had been interpreted by those to whom the preservation of same had been committed.

Hence we find Phinehas and the companion, both having received the experience similar to that received by Hannah and Elkanah, had drawn aside from many of the other groups.

76

And then as in answer to that promise, the child—Judy—was born.

That the entity was a daughter, rather than being a male, brought some disturbance, some confusion in the minds of many.

Yet the life, the experiences of the parents had been such, that still—fulfilling their promise—they brought the life of their child, Judy, and dedicated it to the study and the application of self to the study of those things that had been handed down as a part of the EXPERIENCES of those who had received visitations from the unseen, the unknown—or that worshiped as the Divine Spirit moving into the activities of man.

Hence we find the entity Judy was brought up in that environment; not of disputations, not of argumentations, but rather as that of rote and writ—as was considered necessary for the development, the influences, the activities of the life, to induce or to bring about those experiences.

That much had been to that period as tradition rather than as record, appeared—from the activity of the entity, Judy—to have made a great impression.

So there was the setting about to seek means and manners for the preservation, and for the making of records of that which had been handed down as word of mouth, as tradition. Such channels and ways were sought out. And eventually the manner was chosen in which records were being kept in Egypt rather than in Persia, from which much of the tradition arose, of course, because of the very indwelling of the peoples in that land.

Hence not only the manners of the recording but also the traditions of Egypt, the traditions from India, the conditions and traditions from many of the Persian lands and from many of the borders about same, became a part of the studies and the seeking of the entity Judy early in the attempts to make, keep and preserve such records.

The manners of communication being adverse, owing to the political situations that gradually arose due to the Roman influence in the land, made more and more a recluse of the entity in its early periods; until there were those visitations by what ye call the Wise Men of the East—one from Persia, one from India, one from the Egyptian land.

These reasoned with the Brethren, but more was sought from the studies of the entity Judy at that experience.

Then there was the report by the Wise Men to the king. Has it been thought of, or have you heard it reasoned as to why the Wise Men went to Herod, who was only second or third in authority rather than to the Romans who were ALL authority in the land?

Because of Judy; knowing that this would arouse in the heart and mind of this debased ruler—that only sought for the aggrandizement of self—such reactions as to bring to him, this despot, turmoils with those then in authority.

Why? There was not the proclamation by the Wise Men, neither by Judy nor the Essenes, that this new kind was to replace Rome! It was to replace the Jewish authority in the land!

Thus we find, as it would be termed in the present, attention was called or pointed to the activity of the Essenes such that a little later—during those periods of the sojourn of the Child in Egypt because of same—Herod issued the edict for the destruction.

This brought to those that were close to the entity those periods that were best described by the entity itself, in the cry of Rachel for her children that were being born into a period of opportunity—yet the destructive forces, by the very edict of this tyrant, made them as naught.

Hence during those periods of the ministry of John, and then of Jesus, more and more questioning was brought upon the recorder—or Judy—by the Roman authorities, or the Roman spies, or those who were the directors of those who collected and who registered taxes of those peoples for the Roman collection.

Consequently, we find the entity came in contact with the Medes, the Persians, the Indian influence or authority . . . because of the commercial association

78

as well as the influence that had been upon the world by those activities of Saneid and those that were known during the periods of Brahma and Buddha.

These brought to the experience of the entity the weighing of the counsels from the traditions of the Egyptians and of her own kind—and then that new understanding.

Hence we find the entity in those periods soon after the Crucifixion not only giving comfort but a better interpretation to the Twelve, to the Holy Women; an understanding as to how Woman was redeemed from a place of obscurity to her place in the activities of the affairs of the race, of the world, of the empire—yea, of the home itself.

Those all became a part of the entity's experiences during that portion.

Hence we find many have been, many are, the contacts the entity has made and must make in this present experience.

For, as then, the evolution of man's experiences is for the individual purpose of becoming more and more acquainted with those activities in the relationships with the fellow man, as an exemplification, as a manifestation of Divine Love—as was shown by the Son of man, Jesus; that EACH and every soul MUST BECOME, MUST BE, the SAVIOR of some soul! to even COMPREHEND the purpose of the entrance of the Son INTO the earth—that man might have the closer walk with, yea, the open door to, the very heart of the living God!

The entity's activities during the persecutions aroused much in the minds of those that made war again and again upon the followers of the Nazarene, of Jesus, of the Apostles here and there.

And the entity, as would be termed, was hounded, yea, was persecuted the more and more; yet remaining until what ye would call the sixty-seventh year AFTER the Crucifixion; or until Time itself began to be counted from same.

For the records as were borne by the entity, it will be found, were BEGUN by the activities of the entity

79

during what ye would term a period sixty years AF-
TER the Crucifixion.

And then they were reckoned first by the peoples
of Carmel, and then by the brethren in Antioch, then
a portion of Jerusalem, then to Smyrna, Philadelphia,
and those places where these were becoming more
active.

The entity—though receiving rebuffs, yea, even
stripes in the body—died a natural death in that experience; at the age then of ninety-one.

As to the associations, the lessons that are to be
gained in the applications of self from that experience:

Many are the urges that arise, as indicated; many
are the impluses oft to feel that the very knowledge
puts self in a position to condemn.

But condemn not, even as He did not condemn.

Again there are the inclinations that arise for
abilities to present, to correlate, subjects that are
truths hidden in tradition, hidden in prejudice of
race, hidden in tradition of the patriotic influences
that are accredited by the very spirit of a nation of
people, or a custom, or a condition that has set itself
in order as organizations.

But gathering these, do not condemn. For know,
there is only ONE SPIRIT—that is the Spirit of
Truth that has growth within same! For if there is the
spirit of strife, or the spirit of any activities that bring
about contention or turmoils, it takes hold upon
those very fires that ye have so WELL put away; yet
that keep giving—giving—urges that are spoken of,
even as He that ye KNOW, that the prince of this
world is as a raging lion, going about seeking whom
he may destroy!

What is this spirit then of unrest but that very cry,
as He gave in that triumphal entry, "If ye did not cry
Hosanna, glory to the Lord, the King of Kings, the
very stones would cry out!"

(1472-3; November 18, 1937)

*Q-13. Give a detailed description for literary
purposes, of the choosing of Mary on the temple
steps.*

A-13. The temple steps—or those that led to the altar, these were called the temple steps. These were those upon which the sun shone as it arose of a morning when there were the first periods of the chosen maidens going to the altar for prayer; as well as for the burning of the incense.

On this day, as they mounted the steps all were bathed in the morning sun; which not only made a beautiful picture but clothed all as in purple and gold.

As Mary reached the top step, then, then there were the thunder and lightning, and the angel led the way, taking the child by the hand before the altar. This was the manner of choice, this was the showing of the way; for she led the others on this particular day.

Q-14. *Was this the orthodox Jewish temple or the Essene temple?*

A-14. The Essenes, to be sure.

Because of the adherence to those visions as proclaimed by Zacharias in the orthodox temple, he (Zacharias) was slain even with his hands upon the horns of the altar.

Hence those as were being here protected were in Carmel, while Zacharias was in the temple of Jerusalem.

Q-15. *Was Mary required to wait ten years before knowing Joseph?*

A-15. Only, you see, until Jesus went to be taught by others did the normal or natural associations come; not required—it was a choice of them both because of their own feelings.

But when He was from without the roof and under the protection of those who were the guides (that is, the priests), these associations began then as normal experiences.

Q-16. *Were the parents of John the Messenger members of the band which prepared for Jesus?*

A-16. As has just been indicated, Zacharias at first was a member of what you would term the orthodox priesthood. Mary and Elizabeth were members of the Essenes, you see; and for this very reason

81

Zacharias kept Elizabeth in the mountains and in the hills. Yet when there was the announcing of the birth and Zacharias proclaimed his belief, the murder, the death took place.

Q-17. Where was the wedding performed? of Mary and Joseph?

A-17. In the temple there at Carmel.

Q-18. Where did the couple live during the pregnancy?

A-18. Mary spent the most of the time in the hills of Judea, a portion of the time with Joseph in Nazareth. From there they went to Bethany to be taxed, or to register—as ye would term.

Q-19. Who assisted as midwife?

A-19. This has been touched upon through these sources; and as the daughter of the Innkeeper and those about assisted and aided, these have seen the glory, much, in their experiences.

(5749-8; June 21, 1937)

Q-2. What is the correct meaning of the term "Essene"?

A-2. Expectancy.

Q-3. Was the main purpose of the Essenes to raise up people who would be fit channels for the birth of the Messiah who later would be sent out into the world to represent their Brotherhood?

A-3. The individual preparation was the first purpose. The being sent out into the world was secondary. Only a very few held to the idea of the realization in organization, other than that which would come with the Messiah's pronouncements.

Q-4. Were the Essenes called at various times and places Nazarites, School of the prophets, Hasidees, Therapeutae, Nazarenes, and were they a branch of the Great White Brotherhood, starting in Egypt and taking as members Gentiles and Jews alike?

A-4. In general, yes. Specifically, not altogether. They were known at times as some of these; or the Nazarites were a branch or a THOUGHT of same, see? Just as in the present one would say that any denomination by name is a branch of the Christian-

Protestant faith, see? So were those of the various groups, though their purpose was of the first foundations of the prophets as established, or as understood from the school of prophets, by Elijah; and propagated and studied through the things begun by Samuel. The movement was NOT an Egyptian one, though ADOPTED by those in another period—or an earlier period—and made a part of the whole movement.

They took Jews and Gentiles alike as members,—yes.

Q-5. Please describe the associate membership of the women in the Essene brotherhood, telling what privileges and restrictions they had, how they joined the Order, and what their life and work was.

A-5. This was the beginning of the period where women were considered as equals with the men in their activities, in their abilities to formulate, to live, to be channels.

They joined by dedication—usually by their parents.

It was a free will thing all the way through, but they were restricted only in the matter of certain foods and certain associations in various periods —which referred to sex, as well as to the food or drink.

Q-6. How did Mary and Joseph first come in contact with the Essenes and what was their preparation for the coming of Jesus?

A-6. As indicated, by being dedicated by their parents.

Q-7. Please describe the process of selection and training of those set aside as holy women such as Mary, Editha, and others as a possible mother for the Christ. How were they chosen, were they mated, and what was their life and work while they waited in the Temple?

A-7. They were first dedicated and then there was the choice of the individual through the growths, as to whether they would be merely channels for general services. For, these were chosen for special services at various times; as were the twelve chosen at the time, which may be used as an illustration. Remember, these came down from the periods when the school had begun, you see.

When there were the activities in which there were to be the cleansings through which bodies were to become channels for the new race, or the new preparation, these then were restricted—of course—as to certain associations, developments in associations, activities and the like. We are speaking here of the twelve women, you see—and all of the women from the very beginning who were dedicated as channels for the new race, see?

Hence the group we refer to here as the Essenes, which was the outgrowth of the periods of preparations from the teachings by Melchizedek, as propagated by Elijah and Elisha and Samuel. These were set aside for preserving themselves in direct line of choice for the offering of themselves as channels through which there might come the new or the divine origin, see?

Their life and work during such periods of preparation were given to alms, good deeds, missionary activities—as would be termed today.

Q-8. Please tell of the contacts of Thesea, Herod's third wife, with the Essenes, her meeting with one of the Essene Wise Men, and what were the names of the two wives preceding her?

A-8. There was the knowledge of same through the giving of information by one of those in the household who had been so set aside for active service. Through the manner and conduct of life of that individual, and the associations and activities, the entity gained knowledge of that group's activities.

Q-9. Please describe the Essene wedding, in the temple, of Mary and Joseph, giving the form of ceremony and customs at that time.

A-9. This followed very closely the forms outlined in Ruth. It was not in any way a supplanting but a cherishing of the sincerity of purpose in the activities of individuals.

When there was to be the association, or the wedding of Joseph and Mary,—Mary having been chosen as the channel by the activities indicated upon the stair, by the hovering of the angel, the enunciation to Anna and to Judy and to the rest of those in charge of the preparations at that time,—then there was to be sought out the nearer of kin, though NOT kin in the blood relationships. Thus the lot fell upon Joseph, though he was a much older man compared to the age ordinarily attributed to Mary in the period. Thus there followed the regular ritual in the temple. For, remember, the Jews were not refrained from following their rituals. Those of the other groups, as the Egyptians or the Parthians, were not refrained from following the customs to which they had been trained; which were not carried on in the Jewish temple but rather in the general meeting place of the Essenes as a body-organization.

(254-109; May 20, 1941)

. . . Then there were the divers groups, as well as the Essenes, that had set themselves as a channel through which there was expected to be the fulfilling in that particular period of those promises indicated from the first promise to Eve unto the last as had been recorded by Malachi. These were individuals who in their activities of daily life were in keeping with neither of the first indicated groups. Then there were those of the Grecian and Roman faiths, who held to that idea of glorifying the body itself as a channel through which there might be sought manifestation by the divine—if there was a choice made by the divine, or if there were the divine (according to their reasoning).

. . . This entity then came into activity in that heterogeneous or conglomerate thought,—in the name then Ulai. The parentage of the entity was one Archaus—a close adherent of the Essenes' thought yet of the orthodox group—and of one (the mother) who was a close associate of the mother of Martha, Mary and Lazarus, in the name Josada.

Then, the entity was brought up in the tenets or schools of thought that had attempted to be a reconstruction of the former activities established by Elijah in Mount Carmel.

Hence, coming under the influence of ALL of these tenets, the entity was greatly confused through its early experience. The entity had the greater teachings, or was acquainted with the greater teachings of the Carmelites—now the Essenes—and of the orthodox groups that held to the service in the temple and the close associations with these of the students and exponents of the Roman and Grecian people. It was to these latter mentioned teachings that the entity turned more, in its early years.

Thus when there were the first presentations to the entity of the thought as to the teachings of the Nazarene, and the entity having rejected John as a disciple or even a forerunner, these appeared as mysteries to the entity.

Hence oft in its activities the entity grew cold, and again very enthusiastic as to the varying forms of activities—both as to the social and as to the more strict religious groups. (993-5; February 19, 1941)

The Essenes were a group of individuals sincere in their purpose, and yet not orthodox as to the rabbis of that particular period. Thus such a meeting would be described by the meditations, certain ritualistic formulas, as may be outlined very well from some of those activities as may be gathered from the activities of the priest in the early period when there was the establishing of the tabernacle.

Remember, recall, the first two didn't do so well, even under the direction of the high priest; for they offered strange fire.

Let not, then, that as would be offered here, become as strange fire, but as in keeping with the precept of Jesus, "I and the Father are one"; not individually, but in the personal application of the tenets, commandments, being one in purpose, one in application.

Thus such a meeting would be the interpreting of each promise that has been made; as to when, as to how there would come the Promised One.

Analyze in the mind, then, that from the 3rd of Genesis through to the last even of Malachi. Set them aside. Use them as the basis of discussions, as the various groups may be set in order; each rotating as a teacher, as an instructor for that particular meeting; remembering all were secret meetings.

Q-4. Tell of the work, the prophecies, the hopes of Phinehas and Elkatma, Judy's parents, at Carmel, as Essenes.

A-4. These were those activities that may be illustrated very well in the ministry of the parents of the strong man—that a parallel may be drawn; as to how first there was the appearance to the mother, and then the father, as to what should be the ministry, the activity of the entity that was to lead that group, and aid in the early teaching of the prophecies of the life of the child Jesus, as well as of John. For, John was more the Essene than Jesus. For Jesus held rather to the spirit of the law, and John to the letter of same.

Q-17. Please describe Judy's home life as well as her Essene activities.

Q-17. That as might be the description of an individual who had set self aside as a channel for such activities. These are very hard to be understood from the material mind, or from the material understanding or concept, especially in this period of consciousness. For, then man walked close with God. When there were those preparations—it is possible in the present, but not ACCEPTABLE. Consequently, to describe the home life as to say they sat in the sun, ate three square meals a day and wore little or nothing, or that they dressed in the best—it must be that as from the spirit. May best be described as given by Luke, in his description of those things that disturbed Mary. "She kept these things and pondered them in her heart." This did not prevent her from being, then, a material person, nor one with the faculties and desires for material associations—as indicated in the lack of celibacy. Is this indicated in any condition in the book, or man's relationship to God? Nowhere is this indicated!

Q-18. Tell about Judy teaching Jesus, where and what subjects she taught him, and what subjects she planned to have him study abroad.

Q-18. The prophecies! Where? In her home. When? During those periods from his twelfth to his fifteenth-sixteenth year, when he went to Persia and then to India. In Persia, when his father died. In India when John first went to Egypt—where Jesus joined him and both became the initiates in the pyramid or temple there.

Q-19. *What subjects did Judy plan to have him study abroad?*

A-19. What you would today call astrology.

Q-20. *At what major event in Jesus's life was Judy present, such as casting out of demons, healing, feeding five thousand, etc.?*

A-20. At his teaching—for a period of some five years.

Q-21. *Was she present at any of the healings or the feeding of the multitudes?*

A-21. Those where she chose to, but, she was very old then. She lived to be sufficiently old to know, of course, of the feeding of the first five thousand. She was present but rather as one that brought the crowds together, than as contributing to the activities at the time. For, there the divisions arose, to be sure.

Q-22. *Was Judy present at the Crucifixion or the Resurrection?*

A-22. No. In spirit—that is, in mind—present. For, remember, Judy's experience at that time was such that she might be present in many places without the physical body being there!

(2067-11; February 22, 1943)

DREAM SEMINAR

W. Lindsay Jacob, M.D.

A dream is an attempt on the part of the subconscious of the individual to convey information to his conscious awareness.

88

The foregoing statement reflects much of the general attitude of the Edgar Cayce readings toward dreams. The readings seem to indicate that by utilizing the information presented in one's dreams, the individual can help himself in the physical, mental and spiritual aspects of his life. For many years the A.R.E. has been teaching this point of view on dreams by publishing a great deal of helpful material for analyzing one's own dreams and by conducting summer school sessions in which we have attempted to instruct the students in understanding the information presented to them in their dreams. This paper is both a brief resumé of how we see dreams at the present time and a preliminary report on what seems to me to be an unusually profitable method of self-help in solving one's problems and improving one's character.

This method of self-help has gradually evolved as the result of our experiences with the summer students in the Dream Seminar. I feel it has a great potential in the field of psychiatry, and I foresee it as becoming a type of group therapy that should be much more effective than most of the types currently in use. It not only provides the individual with a situation for dealing with his current problems but also provides him with a tool for resolving future problems. The use of the individual's current dreams as specimens for discussion in the Dream Seminar has definitely assisted him in dealing with current problems. At the same time, from experience he learns to interpret his own dreams and sets up routines for doing this in the future.

I tend to agree with Jung's statement to the effect that the only accurate interpretation of a dream must come from the dreamer himself. He can certainly do this better with the help of suggestions, comments, and questions from outside observers. He can ultimately learn to make a highly accurate and complete interpretation on his own, as our students have repeatedly demonstrated. Frequently when working on his own a student may not, at least initially, get the entire meaning of a single dream; however, with repeated dreams and practice his understanding of the matter in his current dreams gradually narrows down to real insight. The result brings, at times, substantial changes in behavior. He begins to see things more nearly as they are.

My own personal association with this A.R.E. project has been over the past five years. The experience has led to the crystallization of some ideas concerning dreams that I should like to outline. The first and most important concept is the already stated one that emphasizes the communication aspects. A dream is a message from yourself to yourself. It is presented in disguised form *not* for the purpose of obscuring the information but for the purpose of getting the information past the smoke screen of one's beliefs, prejudices, misconceptions and false self-image. Sanity is defined best and most simply as the ability to see things as they are. Most of us are not as entirely sane as we should like to be, or even as we believe ourselves to be. All of us, through the years of experience in living, have developed a set of beliefs, prejudices and a self-image that are usually not entirely in accord with reality. We, for example, tend to think of ourselves as being good-hearted when we are merely generous, wise when we are only erudite, loving when we are merely possessive; and we have developed other distortions in our view of ourselves and the people and circumstances surrounding us. These misconceptions are very dear to us. Without them we would feel stripped, defenseless, inadequate, and possibly even incompetent. Consequently, we cling to them with a tenacity almost as strong as the instinct for survival. We are often convicted by our convictions. Yet, beneath this distorted image, we really do know what the reality is. Our senses function without distortion and their messages are recorded faithfully and without bias. It is only our interpretation of this information, or our understanding of it, that is distorted and biased. Consequently, our subconscious mind, among other things, has a complete and accurate record of our entire life. As it says in the *Rubaiyat*:

The Moving Finger writes; and, having writ,
Moves on: nor all your Piety nor Wit
    Shall lure it back to cancel half a Line,
Nor all your Tears wash out a Word of it.

It is from this, as well as other sources of knowledge, that the material is gleaned for presentation to us in a dream.

When the dream is remembered we are likely to dismiss it as being "silly," the result of a digestive disturbance, etc. Despite the illogical aspects that dreams initially present, as often as not they have a haunting, sometimes disturbing quality that frequently leads us to muse about them in a puzzled way.

Our sleep would not be particularly restful if about one-quarter of it were occupied with our inner-self informing us as to the situation within and about us. I don't imagine we should doze peacefully while an inner voice was telling us that the conditions of the arteries of the heart were growing critical and we were shortly due to have a heart attack. Nor should we slumber too soundly while being told that if we continued this attitude toward our brother it would be most detrimental to us both and probably lead to serious trouble. Yet these two brief examples are illustrative of the type of information that is being conveyed to us in our dreams.

It's not all bad, incidentally. Frequently dreams give us compliments on what we have done or are doing. Often in the presentation of the material itself a solution is strongly implied and even, occasionally, a solution is given. Such is the dream in which a woman sees herself taking off a pair of black gloves and putting on a pair of white ones. She is telling herself to stop her hateful ways of thinking and be more loving in her thoughts. In any event, nature, as usual, has utilized the parable or symbolic form to preserve an uninterrupted night's rest and at the same time to convey vital information. Freud in his "little" book on the interpretation of dreams, published after the major volume, likens the nature of the dream work to that of a night watchman. That is, he quiets all minor disturbances so that the town sleeps, but should a major emergency occur he will waken the townspeople to attend to it. We have all had the dream experience, I'm sure, in which the purpose was to rouse us because the baby was crying, or because there was a fire in the house, and perhaps most often simply because we needed to know and remember the content of that particular dream.

A dream, then, is presented most often in symbolic or parable form. The reasons for this are at least three-fold—with a fourth, what might be called, fringe benefit.

First, symbols tend to preserve the state of sleep. Second, symbols disguise the information initially, *not* to block it from our conscious awareness but to get it through to the conscious awareness. Third, the best way to condense the greatest amount of information into the smallest possible message is to use parables, pictures, symbols, etc. A fourth possible advantage to this form is the fact it presents itself as an intriguing kind of riddle that titillates the imagination, which in turn almost automatically draws us to attempt to solve it. It is interesting to note that the other outstanding example of teaching in parable form is, of course, contained in the Gospels. The Galilean, in His great wisdom, apparently realized the advantages of this method.

A dream, then, immediately presents two levels of information. The first level, which we call the manifest content, consists of that material that we actually see, hear, experience, etc. in the dream itself. It is usually senseless to us if we take it at face value. For example, it certainly doesn't make much sense to start a trip in a railroad car and then find oneself pedaling a bicycle through the woods. This is the manifest content of the dream. The other level of information in a dream is called the latent content and consists of the meaning of the symbols in the manifest content. The latent content of the dream is its real meaning for us. Analysis of the dream and statement of its latent content is known as dream interpretation. In the above example with the trip starting in the railroad car and ending on a bicycle in the woods, a possible interpretation might be that the endeavor the dream represents has started out in a conventional way with plenty of assistance but has or will end with the individual being all alone—possibly somewhat lost and proceeding strictly under his own power.

It is not my purpose to present here a long discussion on the various types of symbols and their meanings. We must leave this for a more intense and prolonged study. I merely wish to highlight some of the general aspects of dreams and dreaming that have come about as the result of our work with the group at A.R.E. I want to mention, however, the use of color in a dream because, in my experience, little has been written about this in most of the standard works, and it is one of the richest sources of information available in dreams. Those which are presented in color frequently have a greater depth of meaning than the usual black and white ones. Each of the colors used has a specific message. The interpretation of the various colors is surprisingly well known to most of us, appearing in many of our figures of speech; such as, I am feeling blue today; he was red with anger; he was green with envy, etc. The meanings of the colors are ancient, in that they generally have the same significance in dreams as that ascribed to them in religious trappings, heraldic emblems, flags, etc. The quality and intensity of the color usually has significance as well. A dirty green is probably a bad indication. Pastel shades usually refer to less intense emotions; whereas, sharp, clear colors, as a rule, refer to more intense emotion or quality of character. Using the color, as well as the rest of the dream, greatly enriches the interpretation. For instance, a dreamer may indicate he is frozen in something by dreaming he is covered with snow. If the snow is colored blue he is, perhaps, frozen in depression.

From our work with dreams has come an attempt to classify them. We feel there are probably three main types, and several others less often encountered.

The first type we call a physical dream, and its latent content refers to a physical condition in the body of the dreamer. This type tends to point out health problems, such as developing ulcers, high blood pressure, kidney conditions, improper diet and even more everyday things such as the need for a laxative, more rest, more exercise, etc.

The second main type we call a mental dream. This particular variety has to do with the problems of everyday living: our attitudes toward ourselves that cause us trouble; our attitudes toward other people or our work that should be revised; a need for money—in general, the usual problems of living that are not physical.

The third main type is called a spiritual dream. It is usually in color and has to do with those attributes of character that are generally termed abstract and yet are somehow most concrete: things such as the quality of our courage; whether we are thinking for good or evil; the intensity of our drive for power; the quality of our charity. Needless to say, very few dreams fall entirely within one category. Most contain elements of at least two of these types.

Other varieties of dreams are precognitive, telepathic, clairvoyant, etc; unusual experiences we call "visions." With respect to the precognitive dream, I want to point out that many dreams are predictive. They indicate trends in our thinking or behavior that will probably result in a specific type of event. This aspect of dreaming is not truly precognitive and merely results from the ability of our subconscious to interpolate ahead from the data at hand. This type of prediction generally is no surprise to us once the dream has been interpreted and usually covers only a relatively short period forward in time—a few weeks to a few months. A truly precognitive dream is generally a complete surprise, and often we are unable to interpret it until after the event has occurred because it has no latent content. It is merely a straightforward presentation of the event that is being predicted.

Telepathic and clairvoyant dreams are usually of the same nature—a straightforward presentation of the facts. However, many dreams contain minor elements of ESP, generally presented in symbolic form. When ESP material is presented in this way it is quite difficult to prove it as such and consequently this aspect of dreaming is, and probably always will be, cloudy and confused.

A vision is usually an intense dream experience that immediately affects the individual to the very depths of his being and as a result cannot be classified as an ordinary dream. There are many fine examples of this type of experience in the autobiographies of religious individuals.

In our work in the Dream Seminars we try to concentrate more on aspects of dreaming defined in these three main categories of dreams, physical, mental and spiritual, as we feel this is the most important and fruitful line of approach for the individual student. The specimen dreams we have worked with have contained some material suggestive of ESP in symbolic form. There have been a very few precognitive dreams that were not recorded by the student during the summer session but at other times in the year.

The Dream Seminar was comprised of six to fifteen students. They were normal individuals whose motivation was good, since a prerequisite for the Seminar was a collection of fifty previously recorded dreams. The atmosphere of the class itself was relaxed and there was little difficulty in getting the students to face issues, and develop insights. Only rarely did the leaders of the Seminar feel it necessary to soft pedal or avoid one or another of the more intensely personal levels of interpretation of the dreams presented. Usually by the end of the one or two week session the students themselves were making good interpretations of their own dreams and as a group were really dissecting in great detail the dreams presented to them. Many of them developed surprising insights into their own characters and attitudes during this very short time we had to spend with them. Many others have informed us by correspondence during the year of how they have been able to continue using what they have learned to further their understanding of themselves and their problems. Many of them have come back more than once because they felt the work to be quite profitable from a personal standpoint.

In addition to the above, during the last summer session we conducted a pilot study to determine whether or not various stimuli might have an effect on the type and quality of the individual's dreams. The students were divided into small groups using various stimuli, most of which were suggested by the Edgar Cayce readings.

In order to obtain as many dreams as possible the students were divided into teams of three, consisting of one observer and two sleepers. The observer would arise at about 3:00 A.M. and awaken the dreamers each time after random eye movements were observed. This technique did increase the number of dreams by about fifty percent over what would ordinarily have been produced in this length of time, judging from past experience. In view of the small numbers used, results were in no way conclusive. Previous studies of dreams indicate that external stimuli usually have little effect on the dream content. Therefore, we did not expect nor find a marked difference in the quality and type of dream in the various groups.

As I have stated before, the most exciting thing about the whole project has been the growing realization that we have here what can obviously be a very effective tool for helping people with clinical problems, as well as normal individuals. In this day and age where the need for psychiatric services seems already to have increased well beyond the capacity of the manpower available to deal with it, such an effective method of helping many people at the same time should not be overlooked.

THE EDGAR CAYCE READINGS ON DREAMS

The following readings on dreams, from the Edgar Cayce records, have been selected as being representative of the premise upon which the more than six hundred dream readings were given. Herein is revealed a purpose and usefulness of the dream which goes far beyond that heretofore advocated by psychology.

While the idea of reincarnation, so prominent in the Edgar Cayce readings, was not new here, the idea of the dream as being a mechanism of interrelated mind activities between the conscious, subconscious and superconscious for soul development was, apparently, new. The dream purpose seems to be to bring to the consciousness an illustration of mind and soul ideals in comparison with conscious willful actions for a directive or helpful influence.

The scope of dream activities seems much broader than heretofore studied, and presents a philosophy of man in the earth; his growth and development or regression; his reincarnating and its purposes; as well as the essence of man himself.

The first answer that had any reference to dreams, was in response to the question:

> Q-4. How can we best develop our sub-conscious minds to be of the most benefit to our

fellow men while in the physical plane of living?

A-4. By developing the mental or physical mind
toward the uplift of mankind toward the Maker, leaving those things behind that so easily beset the
physical body.

By the training of the mental—through the physical forces and the subconscious urge, as we have
given—in the right or direct way, and lending
assistance to the uplift of all.

The THOUGHT held against an individual directs
the mind, either of the masses or classes; whether
toward good or bad. Thought is reached through the
physical forces, and, by becoming a part of the
physical or conscious mind, either lends strength of
subconscious forces, or allows the subconscious to
direct.

Not that the physical mind gives strength, except
by allowing the subconscious to direct, and by not
building barriers [that must then] be overcome.

That [which is] to be overcome might as well be
met in this plane; for it will have to be met eventually,
before we can gain the entrance to the Holy of Holies.

This is the manner in which to train or conduct the
physical to lend the assistance to the subconscious
forces to direct and give the help the world or
populace needs.   3744-1

*Q-41.   Give the best method of helping the human
family increase in knowledge of the subconscious soul
or spirit world.*

A-41.   The knowledge of the subconscious of an
entity of the human family, is as of one integral
force, element, or self in the creation of the human
family; and until the individual makes known to
groups, classes, countries, nations THE GREATER
STUDY OF SELF, that force will only be magnified.
That of the spirit is the spark or portion of the Divine
that is in every entity, whether complete or evolving
to that completeness.

The study (from the human standpoint) of subconscious, subliminal, psychic, soul forces, is and
should be the great study for the human family; for
man will understand its Maker when it understands

its RELATION to its Maker; and it will only understand that THROUGH ITSELF.

That same understanding is the knowledge as is given here in this state.

Each and every person getting that understanding has its individual [obligation] towards the Great Creation, and its individual niche, place, and duty to perform. It has to reach numbers of psychic forces or phenomena that may be manifested in the earth plane.

All the same, the understanding for the individual entity, viewed from its own standpoint and knowledge, is acquired and made ready by ITSELF, to be manifested through itself towards its own development, and hence in that development of the Creation, or world.

Only in this manner and in this form and in this way, will such a development be of assistance to the world. As in DREAM, those forces of the subconscious, when correlated into forms that relate to the various phases of the individual, give to that individual the better understanding of self, when correctly interpreted,

Forget not that it has been said correctly that the Creator; the gods and the God of the Universe; speaks to man through this individual self.

Man approaches the nearer condition to that field when the normal is at rest; in sleep or slumber. And when more of the forces are taken into consideration, and are studied by the individual, (not by someone else), it is EACH individual's job . . . to receive the message from the higher forces themselves, and for EACH individual to [decide whether] he will study to show himself approved. 'In all Thy getting, My Son, get understanding.' That of Self.

When one understands self, and self's relation to his Maker, his duty to his neighbor and his own duty to self, he cannot, will not, be false to man or to his Maker. Give then more thought, FOR THOUGHTS ARE DEEDS, and are children of the relation reached between the mental and the soul. Thought has its relation to the plane of existence of the spirit and the soul, as it does to the physical or earth plane.

What man thinks continually, he becomes; what he cherishes in his heart and mind, he makes a part of the pulsation of his heart through his own blood cells; and he builds, in his own physical, that which his spirit and soul must feed upon, and THAT BY WHICH IT WILL BE POSSESSED when it passes into the realm where the experiences it has gained here in the physical plane MUST be used.

The attributes of the soul and spirit are as many—and as many more!—as the attributes of the physical or mental mind. Each, in the beginning, was endowed with that same condition—position. Each, in itself is building to itself, by means of its development through the ages as they manifest upon the earth plane.

With each development, that force known upon this plane as WILL is given to man over and above all Creation.

THAT FORCE may separate itself from its Maker, for with the WILL man may either adhere to or reject DIVINE LAW—those immutable laws which are set between the Creator and the created.

Study these; especially through any of those phases wherein the carnal or material or normal forces are laid aside; and the ever-present elements of the spirit and soul commune with those of the forces as found in each entity. Study those and KNOW THYSELF.

Q-43. What is a dream?

A-43. There are many and various kinds of manifestations that come to a being that is in the physical plane of man, [one of] which the human family terms a DREAM.

Some are produced by [such] suggestions as reach the consciousness of the physical in the various forms and manners when the physical, in that region called sleep or slumber, has laid aside the conscious.

When those forces through which the spirit and soul have manifested themselves are re-enacted by this same soul and spirit force (in such a manner) as to convey or bring back impressions to the conscious mind in the earth plane; it is termed a dream.

99

This may well be caused by those forces that are taken into the system. The action of digestion that takes place under the guidance of subconscious forces becomes a part of that plane through which the spirit and soul of the entity pass at such time. Such manifestations are termed or called nightmares, or the abnormal manifestations on the physical plane of these forces.

In the normal course of dreams, those forces are enacted that may be the FORESHADOWS of a condition, when the soul and spirit force compares the conditions in various spheres through which (the soul and spirit of) a given entity has passed in its evolution to its present sphere.

In this age at present, 1923, there is not sufficient credence given dreams; for the best development of the human family is to give the greater increase in knowledge of the subconscious soul or spirit world. This is a DREAM.

Q-44. How should dreams be interpreted?

A-44. Depending upon the physical condition of the entity, and that which produces or brings the dream to that body's forces. The better definition is this: correlate those truths that are enacted in each and every dream that becomes a part of the entity of the individual, and use such (for the purpose of) better development; ever remembering that 'develop' means going TOWARD the higher forces, or the Creator.   3744-4

In the intervening years, many individual dreams were interpreted by Edgar Cayce, but it was not until 1932 that this specific question brought the following definitive answer.

Mrs. C: You will please outline clearly and comprehensively the material which should be presented to the general public in explaining just what occurs in the conscious, subconscious and spiritual forces of an entity while in the state known as sleep.

Mr. C: While there has been a great deal written and spoken regarding experiences of individuals in that state called sleep, there has only recently been the attempt to control or form any definite idea of what produces conditions in the unconscious (subconscious, subliminal or subnormal) mind. [These are] attempts to determine that which produces the CHARACTER of the dream as experienced by an individual or entity.

Such experiments may determine—for some minds —questions respecting the claim of some psychiatrist or psychoanalyst; and, through such experiments, refute or determine the value of such [claims] by the study of certain character of mental disturbances in individuals. Yet little of this may be called true analysis of what happens to the body—either physical, mental, subconscious or spiritual—when it loses itself in such repose.

To be sure, there are certain definite conditions that take place respecting the physical, the conscious, and the subconscious (as well as spiritual) forces of a body. So, in analyzing such a state for a comprehensive understanding, all things pertaining to these various factors must be considered.

First, we would say, sleep is a shadow of that intermission in earth's experiences called death; for the physical consciousness becomes unaware of existent conditions, save those determined by the attributes of the physical which partake of the attributes of the imaginative or the subconscious and unconscious forces of that same body.

That is, in a normal sleep (from the physical standpoint we are reasoning now) the senses are on guard, as it were; so that the auditory forces are those that are the more sensitive . . . So, then, we find that there are left four other attributes that act independently and coordinatingly in awareness for a physical body to be conscious. These, in the state of sleep or repose, have become unaware of that which is taking place about the object so resting.

The organs that are of that portion known as the inactive—those not necessary for conscious movement—keep right on with their functioning, [just] as the pulsations, the heart beat, the assimilating and excretory systems keep right on functioning, [even though] there are periods during such a rest when even the heart and the circulation may be said to be "at rest."

What, then, is *not* in action during such period? That known as the sense of perception, as related to the physical brain.

Hence it may be truly said that the auditory sense is subdivided, and there is the act of hearing by feeling, the act of hearing by the sense of smell, and the act of hearing by *all* the senses that are independent of the brain centers themselves, but are rather of the lymph centers.

Throughout the entire sympathetic system is such an accord as to be MORE aware, MORE acute, even though the body-physical and the brain-physical are in repose, or unaware.

This, the sixth sense, as it may be termed for consideration here, partakes of the ACCOMPANYING ENTITY that is ever on guard before the throne of the Creator itself.

It is that that may be trained or submerged, or left to its own initiative, until it makes war with the self in some manner or expression—which must show itself in a material world as in dis-ease, or disease, or temper, or any form that has enabled the brain to become so altered as to respond much in the manner that a string vibrates to certain sound [according to the way] it is strung or played upon. This sense that governs such may be known as the OTHER SELF of the entity or individual. Hence we find there must be some definite line that may be taken by that OTHER SELF; and much has been recorded as to certain given effects it may produce—not on the mind, to be sure; for its (area of operation is) outside those in which the mind or the brain-centers are ordinarily known to function—but upon the same individual, nevertheless.

In purely physical sleep we find the body is relaxed—and there is little or no tautness within same. [It is then that] those involuntary activities that function through the organs that are under the supervi-

sion of the subconscious or unconscious self UNITE
with those forces that have been acted upon by that
which the body has fed upon. Then it may be seen that
the same body, fed upon meats for a period—[as
against] the same body fed upon only herbs and
fruits—would not [supply] the same character or activity to the OTHER SELF, in its activity, as that
called the DREAM SELF. Nor does it produce the
same effect upon any other individual sharing the
same environment under the same circumstances.

This should lead one to know, to understand, that
there is a definite connection between that which we
have chosen to term the sixth sense—acting through
the auditory forces of the body-physical—and the
OTHER SELF within self.   5754-1

Now, with that as has just been given, that there is
an active force within each individual that functions
in the manner of a sense when the body-physical is in
sleep, repose or rest, we would then outline as to
what are the functions of this we have chosen to call
a sixth sense.

Many words have been used in attempting to
describe what the spiritual entity of a body is, and
what relation this spirit or soul bears to the active
forces within a physical normal body. Some have
chosen to call this the cosmic body . . . that body
with which the individual, or man, is clothed in his
advent into the material plane.

These are correct . . . yet by their very classifica-
tion, by calling them by names to designate their
faculties or functionings, have been limited in many
respects.

But what relation has this sixth sense (as has been
termed in this presented, with this *soul* body, this cosmic consciousness? What relation has it with the
faculties and functionings of the normal physical
mind? Which must be trained? The sixth sense? or
must the body be trained in its other functionings to
the dictates of the sixth sense?

In understanding, then, let's present illustrations as
a pattern, that there may be comprehension of that
which is being presented.

103

This ability or this functioning that is so active when physical consciousness is laid aside—as has been termed by some poet, when the body rests in the arms of Morpheus—leaves a definite impression.

Upon what? The mental activities of the body; or the subconscious portion of the body (which, it has been termed, never forgets); upon the spiritual essence of the body; or upon the soul itself? These are questions, not statements!

This sixth sense activity is the activating power or force of the OTHER SELF. What OTHER SELF? That which has been builded by the entity through its experiences as a whole in the material and cosmic world. Hence does the subconscious make aware to this active force, when the body is at rest, some action on one part of self or another that is in disagreement with . . . that OTHER SELF. Hence we may find that an individual may, from sorrow, sleep—and wake with a feeling of elation. Ever when the physical consciousness is at rest, the OTHER SELF communes with the *soul* of the body, see?

Hence we find the more spiritual-minded individuals are the more easily pacified; [because they are] at peace and in harmony in their normal active state as well as in sleep.

Why? They have set before themselves that which is a criterion that may be wholly relied upon; for that from which an entity or soul sprang is its awareness of the Divine, or the creative forces within its experience.

Hence they that have the Name of the Son have put their trust in Him. He is their standard, their model, their hope, their activity.

On the other hand, oft we find one may retire with a feeling of elation or peace, and wake with a feeling of depression, of being alone, or being without hope, or fear having entered: the body-physical awakes with that depression that manifests itself as of low spirits.

What has taken place?

The components of the soul are meeting that which it has merited, for the purpose of clarifying its association of itself with whatever it has set as its ideal.

If one has set self in array against that of love as manifested by the Creator in the material plane, then there *must* be a continual—continual—warring of those elements.

By comparison, then, we may find how it was that the energy of creation manifested in the Son . . .

. . . What, then, has this to do, you ask, with the subject of sleep? Sleep is that period when the soul takes stock of that which it has acted upon during one rest period to another, drawing—as it were—the comparisons that make for life itself in its *essence*.

As for harmony, peace, joy, love, long-suffering, patience, brotherly love, kindness—these are the fruits of the Spirit.

Hate, harsh words, unkind thoughts, oppressions and the like, these are the fruits of the evil forces (of Satan), and the soul either abhors that through which it has passed, or enters into the joy of its Lord.

Why should this be so in one portion, or one part of a body, rather than another?

How received woman her awareness? Through the sleep of man! Hence intuition is an attribute [achieved by] the suppression of those forces from which it sprang, yet endowed with all of those abilities and forces of its Maker that made for its activity in an aware world—or, if we choose to term it such, a three-dimensional world, a material world, where a being must SEE a materialization to become aware of its existence in that plane.   5754-2

This purpose and function of the dreaming process is to review what has been done and thought with the *ideals* of the higher self; and then to confront the physical conscious self with dream symbols which indicate where it has erred and fallen short, or—less often—made spiritual progress.

As to how the sixth sense may be used, then, depends upon the ideal of the individual; for, as has been so well pointed out in Holy Writ, if the ideal of the individual is lost, then the abilities to contact the spiritual forces are gradually lost, or barriers are builded that prevent the individual from sensing his nearness to a spiritual development.

As to those who are nearer the spiritual realm; their visions, dreams and the like are more often retained by (the waking) individual; for, as is seen as a first law, this is self-preservation.

Self rarely desires to condemn self, save when the selves are warring one with another; as are the elements within a body when eating of that which produces what is termed a nightmare—they are warring with the senses of the body, and partake either of those things that cause fear, or produce visions [of a like nature to] the elements that have been taken within the system.

Then, how may this be used to develop a body in its relationship to the material, the mental, and the spiritual forces? Whether it is the body's desire or not, in sleep the consciousness is physically laid aside.

As to what it will seek, this depends upon what it would associate itself with, physically, mentally, spiritually . . . as has been seen by even those attempting to produce a certain character of vision or dream—these follow another law that is universal . . . Like begets like!

That which is sown in honor is reaped in glory.

That which is sown in corruption cannot be reaped in glory . . . for such experiences as dreams, visions and the like, are but the activities in the unseen world of the real self of an entity.

Q-1. How may one train the sixth sense?

A-1. This has just been given; that which is constantly associated with the mental visioning in the imaginative forces. . . . . THAT will it develop toward. What is that which is and may be sought? When under stress, there are no individuals who haven't at some time been warned of that which may arise in their daily or physical experience. Have they heeded? No! It must be experienced!

106

Q-2.   How may one be constantly guided by the accompanying entity on guard at the Throne?

A-2.   It's as to whether they desire or not! It is there! It doesn't leave, but is the active force!

This might confuse some, for—as has been given—the subconscious and the abnormal, or the "unconscious conscious," is the mind of the soul: that is, (in the sense that this is used) it is the subconscious or subliminal self that is on guard ever with the Throne itself.

For has it not been said: "He has given his angels charge concerning thee, lest at any time thou dashest thy foot against a stone"?

Have you heeded? Then He is near!

Have you disregarded? Then He has withdrawn to thine OTHER SELF, see? That self that has been builded as the companion, that must be presented— that is presented—is before the Throne itself!

Consciousness—man seeks this for his OWN diversion. In sleep he seeks the REAL diversion, or the real activity of self.

Q-3.   What governs the experiences of the astral body while in the fourth dimensional plane during sleep?

A-3.   As has been given, that upon which it has fed; that which it has builded; that which it has sought; that which the mental mind, the subconscious mind, the subliminal mind, *seeks! That* governs.

Then we come to an understanding of "he that would find, must seek."

In the physical or material, this we understand.

It is also the pattern of the subliminal or the spiritual self.

Q-4.   What state or trend of development is indicated if an individual does not remember dreams?

A-4.   The negligence of its associations, both physical, mental and spiritual! Indicates a very negligible personage!

Q-5.   Does one dream continually, but simply fail to remember consciously?

A-5.   There is no difference between the unseen

107

world and that which is visible; save that in the unseen, so much greater expanse or space may be covered!

Does one always desire to associate itself with others? Do individuals always seek companionship in this or that period of their experiences in each day? Do they withdraw themselves? That desire lies, or carries on! See? It's a natural experience, not unnatural!

Don't seek for unnatural or supernatural!

It is the natural—it is nature—it is God's activity! HIS associations with man, HIS desire to make for man a way towards an understanding!

If there could be seen or understood fully that illustration given of the Son of man—that while those in the ship were afraid because of the elements, the Master of the sea and the elements slept!

What associations may there have been with that sleep? Was it a natural withdrawing?

Yet when spoken to, the sea and the winds obeyed His voice.

Thou may do even as He, wilt thou but make thineself aware . . .

Q-6. Is it possible for a conscious mind to dream while the astral or spirit body is absent?

A-6. A conscious mind, while the body is absent, is as one's ability to divide self and do two things at once; as is seen by the activities of the mental mind.

The ability to read music and play [it at the same time] is using different faculties of the same mind.

Then, for one faculty to function while another is functioning in a different direction is not only possible but probable; dependent upon the ability of the individual to concentrate, or to centralize in their various places those functionings, of the spiritual forces in the material plane. Beautiful, isn't it?

Q-7. What connection is there between the physical or conscious mind and the spiritual body during sleep or during an astral experience?

A-7. As has been given, a SENSING! With what? That separate sense, the ability of sleep that makes for acuteness with those forces in the physical being that are manifest in everything animate.

As the unfolding of the rose—the quickening in the womb of the grain as it buds forth—the awakening in all nature of that which has been set by the Divine forces to make for an awareness of its presence in *matter,* or material things.   5754-3

A whole new concept of man in the earth is presented in these answers; in that physical consciousness is a *diversion* of man's essential activity—the *real* entity exists at the subconscious level.

KARMA—OUR JOT AND TITTLE

Mary Ann Woodward

For verily I say unto you, till heaven and earth pass, one jot or one tittle shall in no wise pass from the law, till all be fulfilled.

Matt. V:18

And it is easier for heaven and earth to pass, than one tittle of the law to fail.

Luke XVI:17

The immutable law mentioned in these references from the New Testament is the law of cause and effect, the law of karma. The term "karma" comes from a Sanskrit word which means action and reaction. In Hinduism it connotes the labor of the soul, seeking to attain union with God. Edgar Cayce explained karma in its many aspects and ramifications as "meeting self."

Most of our acts produce an immediate result of which we are usually aware. However, many circumstances or conditions we meet seem to have no cause for which we are responsible in the present, and often in misery we cry out as did Job, "Why has this been visited upon me?"

The theory of reincarnation, which holds that man lives many times in the earth, has as its very core the implication that effects which are felt in a present life often have their causes in previous ones. Many people see in this belief the only explanation for the inequalities in the world; for the startling contrast in the conditions into which people are born. The Edgar Cayce readings maintain that each person is responsible for the circumstances in which he finds himself and explain that if he chooses to consider himself an innocent victim of his environment or experiences, it is simply because he lacks a depth of understanding.

What ye sow, ye reap. There are often experiences in which individuals apparently reap that which they have not sown, but this is only the short self vision of the entity or the one analyzing and studying purposes or ideals in relationship to those particular individuals. 2528-3

Meeting self, according to the information in the readings, is actually meeting the results of our own actions or attitudes. An acceptance of reincarnation implies the acceptance of the fact that each individual faces results he brought about. Not only do we make daily choices for which we are responsible, but we have made choices in previous lives for which we are responsible. We are free to choose, but we must realize that within each choice are future choices. The consequences of our choices and acts are the "jot and tittle" that we must face.

Cause and effect to many are the same as karma. Karma is that brought over, while cause and effect may exist in the one material experience only. 2981-21

A-1. *Most* individuals in the present misinterpret karmic conditions. The development or destiny as karmic influences—each soul, each entity, should gain the proper concept of destiny. Destiny is within, or is as of faith, or is as the gift of the Creative Forces. Karmic influence is, then, rebellious influence against such. When opportunities are presented, it is the entity's own *will* force that must

110

be exercised—that which has separated it or has made it equal to the creative influences in the higher spiritual forces to make for itself that advancement. Then in *every* contact is there the opportunity for an entity, a soul, to fulfill or meet in itself or its soul self's association with the Creative Forces from the First Cause, to embrace that necessary for the entity to enter into the at-oneness with that Creative Force. Hence as for the entity's fulfilling, it is *ever* on the road.   903-23

For Life and its expressions are one. Each soul or entity will and does return, or cycle, as does nature in its manifestations about man; thus leaving, making or presenting—as it were—those infallible, indelible truths that it—Life—is continuous. And though there may be a few short years in this or that experience, they are one; the soul, the inner self being purified, being lifted up, that it may be one with that first cause, that first purpose for its coming into existence.

And though there may be those experiences here and there, each has its relationships with that which has gone before, that is to come. And there has been given to each soul that privilege, that choice, of being one with the Creative Forces. And the patterns that have been set as marks along man's progress are plain. *None* mount higher than that which has been left in Him who made that intercession for man, that man through Him might have the advocate with the Father. And those truths, those tenets—yea, those promises—that have been set in Him, are true; and may be the experience of each and every soul, as each entity seeks, strives, tries, desires to become and pursues the way of becoming with Him.

Then, as there has been and is the passage of a soul through time and space, through this and that experience, it has been and is for the purpose of giving more and more opportunities to express that which justifies man in his relationships one with another; in mercy, love, patience, long-suffering, brotherly love.

111

For these be the fruits of the spirit, and they that
would be one with Him must worship Him in spirit
and in truth.   938-1

We and we alone are responsible for what we are and
our condition in this earth.

The Edgar Cayce readings indicate that the individuality is the sum total of what the entity has done about
Creative and ideal forces in its various experiences in the
earth. The individuality changes as the entity acts, thinks,
and feels in the present about its ideals, its experiences,
and its opportunities. Problems, conditions, individuals,
all cause a reaction in the individuality. Each phase of the
entity has its separate attributes, which may be both
physical and spiritual. Also, they may be one, and to accomplish this the entity must use the mind. The mind is
the builder, the way in which one approaches either infinity or materiality.

For, it is not by chance that each entity enters, but
that the entity—as a part of the whole—may fill that
place which no other soul may fill so well.

Thus with each material manifestation there is an
undertaking by an entity to so manifest that it, as a
part of the whole, may become more and more attuned to that consciousness, and thus glorify Him in
the entity's relationships to others in any and in every
experience.

Thus the urges latent or manifested are expressions of an entity in the varied phases of consciousness. In the material or earthly sojourn these
find expressions or manifestations in a three-
dimensional manner. Each entity, thus, finds itself
body, mind and soul. These phases represent the
three spiritual attributes that are understandable or
comprehended in materiality. Yet as the mental and
the spiritual become more and more expressive, or
controlling through the experiences in the earth, the
entity becomes aware of other dimensions in its
material sojourn.

While body is subject to all the influences of
materiality, it may be controlled—the emotions

thereof—by the mind. And the mind may be directed by spirit. Spirit is that portion of the First Cause which finds expression in all that is everlasting in the consciousness of mind OR matter.

And no urge—whether of the material sojourns or of the astrological aspects—surpasses the mental and spiritual abilities of a soul to choose its course that it, the soul and mind, may take.

In materiality, then, as may be expressed in whatever environ a body has chosen, it becomes accustomed or attuned to the environs of that particular sphere of activity. Yet these may become localized; or they may become state or nation-minded, or spiritual or fellow-man-minded, thereby altering the manner in which the entity may express itself, though under the same environ of others in that particular sphere of activity.   2533-1

Each entity, each soul, enters the material experience for purposes. These are not individual or of a selfish nature, though they are very personal in their application and their practice.

Each soul meets CONSTANTLY ITSELF; not alone in what is called at times karma or karmic influences. For remember, Life is God; that which is constructive grows, that which is destructive deteriorates.

Then, Karmic Forces—if the life application in the experience of an individual entity GROWS to a haven of peace and harmony and understanding; or ye GROW to Heaven, rather than going to heaven, ye grow in grace, in understanding.

Remember then as this: There are promises made by the Creative Forces, or God to the children of men, that "If ye will be my daughter, my son, my child, I will indeed be thy God."

This is an individual promise. Hence the purposes are for an entrance; the SOUL may be prepared for an indwelling with the soul, the mind, of the living God.

How, then, ye ask, are ye to know when ye are on the straight and narrow way?

My Spirit beareth witness with thy spirit that ye are indeed the children of God.

How? Thy God-consciousness, thy soul, either condemns, rejects, or falters before conditions that exist in the experience of the mental and material self. Mind ever is the builder.   1436-1

We often feel we are treated unjustly or that we deserve better things. This is probably only the short view, for we do reap what we sow. We must meet in the physical what we have done in the physical and we meet in the mental what we have done or thought in the mental.

So we have or meet those various aspects in the experience of each individual; for where there has been the constructive or destructive aspects in the experience of each individual, they must be met in that same sphere or plane of activity in which they have been in action in the experience of the entity—and met according to that which is to be meted. For what saith the law? As ye mete, so shall it be meted to thee in thine *own* experience, in thine own activity. So, as individuals in their material or mental experience in the material world find that they are in the activity of being mistreated, as from their angle, from their own angle have they mistreated. If harshness has come to thine own experience, so has there been in thine own activity that which makes for same; and so is the experience in each phase.   262-81

Learn this lesson well—the spiritual truth: Criticize not unless ye wish to be criticized. For with what measure ye mete it is measured to thee again. It may not be in the same way, but ye cannot even THINK bad of another without it affecting thee in a manner of destructive nature.

Think WELL of others and if ye cannot speak well of them don't speak at all—but don't think it either!

Try to see self in the other's place. This will bring the basic spiritual forces that must be the prompting influence in the experience of each soul, if it would grow in grace, in knowledge, in understanding; not

114

only of its relationship to God, its relationship to its fellow man, but its relationships in the home and in the social life.

For know that the Lord thy God is One. And all that ye may know of good must first be within self. All ye may know of God must be manifested through thyself. To hear of Him is not to know. To apply and live and be like Him IS to know!   2936-2

We are constantly meeting ourselves.

For each soul must meet in its own self that which the entity or body metes to its fellow man in "its" ideal relations with such.   876-1

Some may ask, some may say, how or when does one become aware of that mercy, grace? As the individual in the Christ is under the law of grace and mercy and not of sacrifice. Then indeed does each soul, each individual, in same become aware of the saving grace—or the purpose for which the Holy One gave within self that sacrifice such that all through Him may become aware, in the *spiritual* plane, through the grace of the Christ, of the manner in which the individual has met in the material. For He has forgiven thee already. Only in thine brother—as ye are to be judged before Him by the deed done in the body-physical. For once for all has He entered in that ye are forgiven by Him already.   261-81

Have ye not read as He gave, that he who is guilty of one jot or tittle is guilty of it all? Have ye not read that ye shall pay to the uttermost farthing? Yet it is not the same as considered by some, that ye have builded thine own karma—and that the blood, the debt, the law of grace is of none effect. But as He has given, if thine activity is made that ye may be seen of men, or if thine purpose, thine aim, thine desire is for self-glorification, then ye are none of His. Then, the meeting of the deeds done in the body is by relying upon the faith in Him; the activity that makes for an exemplification in the flesh of that faith, of that mer-

115

cy. If ye would have mercy, be ye merciful. If ye would be faithful, show thyself by thy acts that ye trust in Him. How readest thou? "Consider the lilies of the field, how they grow; they toil not, neither do they spin; yet I say unto you that even Solomon in all his glory was not arrayed like one of these." Hast thou put on the Christ, then, in thy activity with thy neighbor, with thy brother, with those of thine own house? Know ye within thyself. Hast thou met with Him in thine inner chamber of thine own temple? Ye *believe* that your body is the temple of the living God. Do ye act like that? Then begin to put same into practice, making practical application of that thou hast gained, *leaving* the results with thy God.

Thou believest He is able to keep that thou hast committed unto Him. Dost thou like that? Dost thou cherish the thought: *"I am in Thy hands. In Thee, O God, do we live and move and have our being in the flesh: And we as Thy children will act just that?"* Speakest thou evil of thy friend, thy foe; or as thou wouldst speak if thou wert in the presence of thy God? Ye are continually in that presence, within thy self. He with the Father, He in thee. Will ye keep the faith that is accounted to thee for righteousness, that thy body in its purging—through the varied experiences in the earth—may *ever* be a channel that points to the living God?

What will ye do about same?   262-82

Actually our karma has many aspects and ramifications reaching into the past and also into the future, if the condition or problem has not been resolved. Not only our acts and deeds, but also our thoughts bring their karmic effects; for thought precedes the deed, and thoughts are things.

"From the abundance of the heart the mouth speaketh"; and thoughts are deeds, and each builds to himself that which is to be glorification, or edification, or resentment built in self. Then act in the way which is befitting and responds in yourself.   294-58

One man asked:

Q-8. Have I karma from any previous existence that should be overcome?

A-8. Well that karma be understood, and how it is to be met. For, in various thought—whether considered philosophy or religion or whether from the scientific manner of cause and effect—karma is all of these and more. Rather it may be likened unto a piece of food, whether fish or bread, taken into the system; it is assimilated by the organs of digestion, and then those elements that are gathered from same are made into the forces that flow through the body, giving the strength and vitality to an animate object, or being, or body. So, in experiences of a soul, in a body, in an experience in the earth. Its thoughts make for that upon which the soul feeds, as do the activities that are carried on from the thought of the period make for the ability of retaining or maintaining the active force or active principle of the thought *through* the experience. Then, the soul re-entering into a body under a different environ either makes for the expending of that it has made through the experience in the sojourn in a form that is called in some religions as destiny of the soul, in another philosophy that which has been builded must be met in some way or manner, or in the more scientific manner that a certain cause produces a certain effect. Hence we see that karma is *all* of these and more. What more? Ever since the entering of spirit and soul into matter there has been a way of redemption for the soul, to make an association and a connection with the Creator, *through* the love *for* the Creator that is in its experience. Hence *this,* too, must be taken into consideration; that karma may mean the development *for self*—and must be met in that way and manner, or it may mean that which has been acted upon by the cleansing influences of the way and manner through which the soul, the mind-soul, or the soul-mind is purified, or to be purified, or purifies itself and hence these changes come about—and some people term it "Lady Luck" or "The body is born under a lucky star." It's what the

117

soul-mind has done *about* the source of redemption of the soul! Or it may be yet that of cause and effect, as related to the soul, the mind, the spirit, the body. 440-5

We often think we have karma with other people as the questioner [1436] in the following interchange did. This is apparently a misunderstanding of the true nature of karma. We only meet ourselves. Karma is a personal thing and only with God or the Creative Forces. It is not between individuals. Other people merely provide the means or conditions for us to learn our lessons and gain self-mastery. We must attain perfection through spiritual unfoldment; so that we may become companions and co-creators with God the Father.

Q-6. Is there some karmic debt to be worked out with either or both and should I stay with them until I have made them feel more kindly toward me?

A-6. Thy relationships to thy fellows through the various experiences in the earth come to be then in the light of what Creative Forces would be in thy relationships to the *act itself*: And whether it be as individual activities to those who have individualized as thy father, thy mother, thy brother or the like, or others, it is merely self being met, in relationships to what they *themselves* are working out, and not a karmic debt *between* but a karmic debt of *self* that may be worked out *between* the associations that exist in the present!

And this is true for every soul.

"If ye will but take that that as was given thee! Neither do I condemn thee—neither do I condemn thee."

WHO GAVE THAT? LIFE ITSELF! Not a personality, not an individual alone; though individually spoken to the entity, to the soul that manifests itself in the present in the name called [1436]. This becomes then not an incident but a *lesson,* that *all* may learn! That is the reason, that is the purpose, that is why in the activity much should be expected, why much shall be endured, why much may be given, by the soul that has learned that God condemns not them that seek to know His face and *believe*!

Then it is not karma but in HIM that the debt is paid.

For who forgave thee thy material shortcomings, thy material errors, as judged by thy superiors at that experience in the material world?

Thy Lord, thy Master—*thyself*! For He stands in thy stead, before that *willingness* of thy inner self, thy soul, to do good unto others; that willingness, that seeking is rightness, if ye will but understand, if ye will but *see*—and *forget* the *law* that killeth but remember the spirit of forgiveness that makes alive! 1436-3

Do not attempt to be good but rather good for *something*!

Know what is thy purpose, what is thy goal! And unless these are founded in constructive, spiritual construction, they will turn again upon thyself!

For each soul is meeting day by day *self*!

Hence as has been given, *know thyself*, in whom thou believest! Not of earthly, not of material things, but mental and spiritual—and *why*! And by keeping a record of self—not as a diary, but thy purposes, what you have thought, what you have desired, the good that you have done—we will find this will bring physical and mental reactions that will be in keeping with the purposes for which each soul enters a material manifestation. 830-3

Every incarnation is an opportunity, so is really good karma whether we are having difficulty in learning our lesson or not. We are attracted to the environment which gives the needed lesson.

We find that there were those environs in which the attraction gave the opportunity for the entity, to bring creative influences and forces in the experience, *to meet self*: and thus correct much that had been and is in the way of development for the soul-entity.

For each soul enters that it may make its path straight. They alone who walk the straight and narrow way may know themselves to be themselves, and yet one with the Creative Forces. Hence the purpose for each entrance is that the opportunities may be embraced by the entity for living, being, that which is creative and in keeping with the Way. For, the Father has not willed that any soul should perish, and is thus mindful that each soul has again—and yet again—the opportunity for making its paths straight. 2021-1

THE THEORY OF OUT-OF-BODY TRAVEL

from the Edgar Cayce Readings

Q-9. Do I actually leave my body at times, as has been indicated, and go to different places?
A-9. You do.
Q-10. For what purpose, and how can I develop and use this power constructively?
A-10. Just as has been given as to how to enter into meditation. Each and every soul leaves the body as it rests in sleep.

As to how this may be used constructively . . . this would be like explaining how one could use one's voice for constructive purposes. It is of the same or of a similar import; that is, it is a faculty, it is an experience, it is a development of the self as related to spiritual things, material things, mental things.

Then as to the application of self in those directions for a development of same . . . it depends upon what is the purpose, what is the desire. Is it purely material? Is it in that attitude, "If or when I am in such and such a position I can perform this or that?" If so, then such expressions are only excuses within self . . . in any phase of an experience.

For as He has given, it is here a little, there a little . . . Use that you have in hand today, *now*, and when

120

your abilities and activities are such that you may be entrusted with other faculties, other developments, other experiences, they are a part of self.

As to how it may be used: Study to show thyself approved unto God, a workman not ashamed of what you think, of what you do, or of your acts; keeping self unspotted from your own consciousness of your ideal; having the courage to dare to do that which you know is in keeping with God's will   853-8

In the following type of out-of-body experience, the "double" was explained.

Q-4. Please explain what took place about February 1935 when while asleep I visited . . . N.C., and talked with an old neighbor. Later this neighbor told others that she had seen me. Should I attempt to develop this type of projection?

A-4. This should be a result and not an attempt; unless ye know for what purpose ye are using same. This has been given in that which has been explained, as to how, for what purpose, what manner, through what channel, for what use, the developments are obtained.

Q-5. Just what type of experience was that which I saw in a dream of several years ago of a tall, light-headed man in a red cape leading a crowd up a hill near . . ., N.C., about August 1, 1935?

A-5. That was of self, or the ability to see self directing that which was and is a portion of the entity's experiences. Learn the lessons from these. In each and every one of thine experiences, as has been indicated, there are the basic truths and purposes and tenets from which lessons may be gained. Have the courage to give these to others!   853-9

An interesting concept may be learned from the following as to being literally "out-of-mind":

Q-3. In certain types of insanity, is there an etheric body involved? If so, how?

A-3. Possession.

121

Let's for the moment use examples that may show what has oft been expressed from here:

There is the physical body, there is the mental body, there is the soul body. They are One, as the Trinity; yet these may find a manner of expression that is individual unto themselves. The body itself finds its own level in its *own* development. The mind, through anger, may make the body do that which is contrary to the better influences of same; it may make for a change in its environ, its surrounding, contrary to the laws of environment or hereditary forces that are a portion of the *Elan vital* of each manifested body, with the spirit or the soul of the individual.

Then, through pressure upon some portion of the anatomical structure that would make for the disengaging of the natural flow of the mental body through the physical in its relationships to the soul influence, one may be dispossessed of the mind; thus ye say rightly, he is *"out of his mind."*

Or, where there are certain types or characters of disease found in various portions of the body, there is the lack of the necessary *vital* for the resuscitating of the energies that carry on through brain structural forces of a given body. Thus disintegration is produced, and ye call it dementia praecox—by the very smoothing of the indentations necessary for the rotary influence or vital force of the spirit within same to find expression. Thus derangements come.

Such, then, become possessed as of hearing voices, because of their closeness to the Borderland. Many of these are termed deranged when they may have more of a closeness to the universal than one who may be standing nearby and commenting; yet they are awry when it comes to being normally balanced or healthy for their activity in a material world.   281-24

Another reading not only bears on the out-of-mind idea but also relates an ordinary type of out-of-body experience:

Q-19.   In 1934, during my last surgical operation when I was thought dead, I traveled out of the body

122

to California, to realms of light. Where did I go really, and what was the meaning and purpose of the experience?

A-19. This was a coordination of experiences the body had seen in the experiences of others; correlated with the edges of more than one experience to which the body had been subjected or subjugated in other experiences. As to place—within self. As to conditions—the many experiences of the entity, both mental *and* spiritual, in the various realms of consciousness.

As to its worth within self—the awareness of the universality of consciousness as may be obtained in the one light that is *all* light.   2067-3

The reading which follows indicates that ideas and concepts of the soul are active in our waking and dreaming consciousness.

Q-1. Is the transmutation of human flesh to flesh divine the real mystery of the Crucifixion and Resurrection? Explain this mystery.

A-1. There is no mystery to the transmutation of the body of Christ. For having attained in the physical consciousness the at-one-ment with the Father-Mother-God, the completeness was such that with the disintegration of the body—as indicated in the manner in which the shroud, the robe, the napkin lay—there was then the taking of the body-physical form.

It was not a transmutation, as of changing from one to another.

Just as indicated in the manner in which the body-physical entered the Upper Room with the doors closed, not by being a part of the wood through which the body passed, but by forming from the ether waves that were within the room, because of a meeting prepared by faith. For as had been given, "Tarry ye in Jerusalem—in the upper chamber—until ye be endued with power from on high."

As indicated in the spoken word to Mary in the garden, "Touch me not, for I have not yet ascended

123

to my Father." The body (flesh) that formed, as seen by the normal or carnal eye of Mary, was such that it could not be handled until there had been the conscious union with the source of all power, of all force.

But afterward—when there had been the first, second, third, fourth and even the sixth meeting—He *then* said: "Put forth thy hand and touch the nail prints in my hands, in my feet. Thrust thy hand into my side and BELIEVE." This indicated the transformation.

For, as indicated, when the soul departs from a body—(this is not being spoken of the Christ)—it has all the form of the body from which it has passed—yet it is not visible to the carnal mind, unless that mind has been, and is, attuned to the infinite. Then it appears, in the infinite, as that which may be handled, with all the attributes of the physical being; with the appetites, until these have been accorded to a unit of activity with the universal consciousness.

Just as it was with the Christ-body: "Children, have ye anything here to eat?" This indicated to the disciples and the Apostles present that this was not transmutation but regeneration, a recreation of the atoms and cells of body that might, through desire, masticate material things—fish and honey (in the honeycomb) were given.

As also indicated later, when He stood by the sea and the disciples and Apostles who saw Him from the distance could not, in the early morning light, discern—but when He spoke, the voice made the impression upon the mind of the beloved disciple such that he spoke, "It is the Lord!" The body had prepared fire upon the earth—fire, water, the elements that make for creation. For as the spirit is the beginning, water combined of elements is the mother of creation.

Not transmutation of flesh, but creation, in the pattern indicated.

Just as when there are those various realms about the solar system in which each entity may find itself

124

when absent from the body, it takes on in those other realms not an earthly form but a pattern—conforming to the same dimensional elements of that individual planet or space.

Q-2. How may I project a counterpart of my conscious awareness to any given place desired, and comprehend or even take part in events there?

A-2. Read what we have just been giving. This is an explanation of how. For it takes first spirit and mind form; and may be aware of the elements in space. For time and space are the elements of man's own concept of the infinite and are not realities as would be any bodily element in the earth—as a tree, a rose, a bird, an animal, as even a fellow being.

Yet, just as a body may in its own material mind visualize, draw a concept of an incident that has happened in time, so may the body in spirit and in spiritual mind project itself, be conscious of elements, be conscious of form, by and through spirit mind—as patterned in a conscious mind.

Mind, then, becomes as a stream, with its upper and lower stratum, with that which moves swiftly or that which is resting upon either spirit or physical being.

These come, then, as flashes to a conscious mind. They may be gradually sustained; just as mind may be projected.

Here we will have an illustration: In a camp near here, near this particular spot or place ye occupy, there has been a gift taken by someone else. There will be a projection of the thought, "This *must be returned!*" and it will be. For here we have the parties to this physical condition existent—right and wrong, good and bad, spirit, mind, body. They are parts of this happening, and it is now being replaced.   2533-8

A later reading goes into a more detailed explanation of the changes which must take place before an entity can manifest in out-of-body form.

For . . . as is seen, the body-physical has the attributes of the physical body, [while] the body-celestial or cosmic body has those attributes of the physical with the cosmic added to same; for all hearing, seeing, understanding, become as *one*.

[Thus] the entity so communicating is able to give the information to one that has laid aside physical being, [because] the operation is through that condition in which the cosmic forces become as [one with] that builded in the soul body—the soul body being that form which the cosmic body [takes] when absent from the physical being.

Yet the ideal or I AM remains with that which has been builded by the experience of the soul through its contact with the various conditions in the astral, cosmic, celestial or through those same in the fleshly body.

Not that man should enter into the shell and live by the whole communication with the astral or cosmic plane; but remember that each experience is as relative to one as to another, and must be lived and acted in that plane through which the experience of the entity, the soul, is passing. [The entity] must ever be up and doing for in the various phases of communication, we always find activity not wholly of the astral plane. Rather seek greater activity in the material plane, through which all action is communicable to the mind [which is the builder] in every individual—see?

Q-2. Now let's study this central body or let's call it etheric body for purpose of clarification. It is clothed with that internal essence or ether that composes this earthly section of space and pushes its way into externalization form of matter. Inside this are integrated each of the elements that compose other celestial sections. Upon leaving this plane, then, and going into the next tier of the circle, this earthly etheric garment would be shed for the [garb] of the next section of world. This process would carry on until the center or core is reached, when the body becomes that of the core—correct?

A-2. Correct, in so far as differentiation may be made in those same various phases as have just been

126

presented. This, as given, reaching to the core, becoming a portion of the center, and yet being an individual in itself, conscious of being the center, and still able to make self one with that center, yet able to act independent *of* the center. Wholly the center and acting only with the center, see? This then, is the final end of each individual soul or being in its evolution to that from which it radiated in the beginning; for through the various phases as have been given we find each building, little by little, line upon line, precept upon precept, becoming one with the whole not the whole within itself, but within itself wholly within the whole. . . . for in the etheric body all hearing is as one, or all noise as one noise, all odor as one odor, all feeling as one feeling—yet each being aware of that which it is and its relation to the whole, even in the way and manner as has been given in that of the etheric, celestial, cosmic or soul body—for this grows on and on.

Q-4. . . . Borderland entities tell us they have actually viewed in disinterested fashion the discarded physical body. How do they see that body? With an etheric brain, says Lodge's son* . . . A psychic apparatus is not necessary to consciousness, except of the external physical kind, I know—I have experienced that, but what is that element in the one force that is capable of awareness of self? Sensuousness is the effect kind of consciousness, whereas the 4th dimensional kind is the causation kind.

A-4. (interrupting) This is correct—and this is wherein each and every individual in the cosmic forces or etheric body, or etheric plane, becomes aware of that [which] it is, and of that [which] it is in relation to all other conditions, in so far as that individual development is towards the whole. For to begin from the first, we have in the material plane the counterpart, pattern or model through which all may be understood in the etheric or in the celestial, terrestrial plane—if we choose to use such terms.

* Sir Oliver Lodge's son Raymond.

In the beginning, we find sensuousness, then, is of the body, an attribute to physical being or to physical consciousness.

In the etheric or in the cosmic body, we find that same condition raised to the causation, rather than sensuous . . . just as the radio in its activity finds that, no matter *where,* the same causation that brings one attunement, brings the same when attuned to that same causation. 900-348

TIME, SPACE AND PATIENCE

from the Edgar Cayce Readings

That the Edgar Cayce readings should have dealt with the mysteries of time and space can surprise no one who has even a passing acquaintance with the philosophy that came through this famous clairvoyant. Surprising, however, is the fact that this philosophy most often equated time and space with patience. The extracts presented here explain this equation, continue the story of man's separation from his Creator, and show the necessity of the finite mind to know the infinite. Here, too, is the reminder that whatever a person has done or may do is permanently recorded.

For, in that creation in which souls of men were given the opportunity to become aware of those forces without themselves, when time and space began, there was given that incentive for each entity, each soul, in whatever environment it might be, to make a manifestation of its (the entity's) awareness of its relationships to the Creative forces or God . . . Thus, irrespective of what the entity has done or may do, there is within itself the record of what it has done, upon the skein of time and space. 2173-1

For to the entity—as to the world—patience is the
128

lesson that each soul must learn in its journey through materiality. And this is a thought for the entity: Time, space, and patience are in the mental realm the same as implied by the expression "Father-God, Son and Holy Spirit"; or as Spirit, Body, Soul. They are expressions of the three-dimensional thought. And in Patience then does man become more and more aware of the continuity of life, of his soul being a portion of the Whole; Patience being the portion of man's sphere of activity in the finite being, as Time and Space manifest the creative and motivative force.   1554-3

First, the continuity of life. There is no time; it is one time; there is no space; it is one space; there is no force; it is one force; other than all force in its various phases and applications of force are the emanations of men's endeavors in a material world to exemplify an ideal of a concept of the creative energy, or God, of which the individual is such a part that the thoughts even of the individual may become crimes or miracles, for thoughts are deeds and applied in the sense that these are in accord with those principles as given. That that one meets must be met again. That [which] one applies will be applied again and again until that oneness, time, space, force, or the own individual is one with the whole, not the whole with such a portion of the whole as to be equal with the whole.   4341-1

Thus, "When ye call I will hear and will answer speedily" becomes not as a tenet or as a saying, but as a *living thing* in thy consciousness. Thus ye find as ye interpret Father, Son and Holy Spirit—and bring it into reality, ye pass in time, in space—through *patience*—into the awareness of the other consciousness, the other phases of experience of self and of those about thee.   3188-1

Time, space, and patience, then, are those channels through which man as a finite mind may become aware of the infinite. For each phase of time, each

129

phase of space, is dependent as one atom upon another. And there is no vacuum, for this, as may be indicated in the universe, is an impossibility with God. Then there is no time, there is no space, when patience becomes manifested in love . . . inasmuch as, and in the same manner you treat your fellow man, you treat your problem, you treat your loved ones, you treat your enemy, you are doing unto your Maker. For he too, is a part in time, in space, of that influence you worship. . . .   3161-1

Individual personality demands that time be considered; yet know, too, in self, that time and space are also manifestations of that universal consciousness ye know as God. In patience ye may find the relationship. Learn patience.   3184-1

The entity has been and is being tried, as in time, in space. It is through patience, through less and less of self, that the entity may become aware not only of its relationships to the Creative Forces or God, but of the manner in which it may contribute the more. Those opportunities have been given through the grace, the love of the Creative Forces; that the life, as it presents itself to the throne of grace or mercy, may be purified in the light of His abiding presence.

3292-1

Not that the individuals in the various appearances are different, for—though they bore different names, different characteristics—they are one, even as the Father, the Son and the Holy Spirit are one; and as time, space and patience are one, when there are the full or complete manifestations of same in the awareness of an entity, of unity, of oneness. But to man has been given that ability to know himself to be himself, and yet one with the Creative Force. But what? Through what? The willingness, the desire to make thy will one with His! . . . Without the shedding of blood there is no remission. Why? For, that separation from the spirit IS blood, and its spirit, its

130

movement is of spirit—and that must be put away.   2246-1

Thus we find His intervention in man's attempt throughout the eons of time and space. For these (time and space) become portions of this three-dimensional plane. And what is the other? Time, Space, Patience! For God has shown and does show us day by day, even as His Son gave, that in Patience we become aware of our souls, of our identity, of our being each a corpuscle as it were in the great body, in the heart, of our God. He has not willed otherwise.

Then what is the Spirit of God? PATIENCE, TIME, and SPACE in the material understanding. This, then, is our first premise: that God IS—in the material experience of man—TIME, SPACE, PATIENCE!

For have not even our own wise ones conceived that those elements between that which is and that which will be are of the same? What? God, the Spirit!

PATIENCE, TIME, SPACE! That we may know ourselves to be His; that our spirits, our souls, bear witness in the things that we do in which we bear witness of HIM. For that which has a beginning must have an ending. Hence rebellion and hate and self-ishness must be wiped away, and *with it* will go sorrow and tears and sadness. For *only* good shall rule. For it is the Spirit of God that will move over the face of the earth . . .   262-114

Yet out of Time, Space, Patience, it is possible for the consciousness of the finite to *know* the infinite. . . . that desire to procreate in self, or to hold selfish interests, has grown—grown—until it is—what did He give?—the prince of this world!   262-115

As the individual entity finds itself body, mind, soul, so are the manifestations in a three-dimensional plane. Hence the concept of the finite is in the realm of cause, effect, and purpose, as in the infinite there is the Father, Son, Holy Spirit. The attaining from the mind to the infinite is through time, space, and

131

patience. All of these phases of a human experience in mind and in materiality should be considered by the entity.   3412-12

Time and space are occupied or are peopled with the elements, or spheres, that become activities for souls or entities in their journey through time and space; seeking that home not built with hands but with the thoughts and with the deeds and with the manners in which we have dealt with our fellow souls, our fellow beings.   1597-1

Each soul, each entity, makes upon time and space—through patience recording same—that as may be indeed the record of the intent and purposes, as well as the material manifestations of the entity through its sojourn in materiality.   1681-1

Also, in the interpretation of the universe, we find that time and space are concepts of the mental mind, as to an interpretation of or a study into the relationships . . . in his material world.   1747-5

. . . For, before *any* condition exists in the finite mind, it has become a past condition, relatively spoken, from the infinite mind. As we have in the earth's sphere, when the light from the planets, or any of the elements in the solar system, cast their shadow, or light, upon the earth's element. For such conditions have passed into space before they can be a conscious condition to the human consciousness. Again, the relative conditions in the earth's plane, or sphere, as related to the spiritual conditions, or laws. For, as would again be sought, one who would understand the infinite mind must approach that with the finite [mind] in such condition as to receive that spiritual insight into such relations, much less conditions.   900-24-A4

. . . as these conditions occur, and as they complete themselves through the study of surrounding forces, the entity gains that knowledge of the pure, the true, the only oneness of the entity's submissive forces to the *I am* within self . . . For with the subconscious forces, we find that called the measure of space and time disappears, and the necessity is for a material life to divide such into units called space and time.   137-8

So man's concept of the Godhead is three-dimensional—Father, Son and Holy Spirit. The . . . activity or the motivating force we find is three-dimensional—time, space, and patience. Neither of these exists in fact, except in the concept of the individual as it may apply to time or space or patience.   4035-1

GENETICS, PAST AND PRESENT

Juliet Brooke Ballard

The Ledger-Star, Norfolk, Va., April 12, 1966:

Los Angeles (AP)—"When ancient Egyptians mummified their pharoahs thousands of years ago, they did so in the belief that the dead would be reincarnated in all their splendor at some future time.

"That time, says a university zoologist, is no more than a century or two away.

"But the process will be reconstitution intead of reincarnation, Professor Elof Carlson told a group of fellow scientists Monday. The actual dead will not be brought back to life, but in their place will be grown physical copies of men and women who once lived, he said.

"The copies will have all of the genius possessed by their predecessors, except for their memories and emotions.

"Prof. Carlson, a zoologist at the University of California at Los Angeles, said the process will be routine within a century or two because of the study of genetic codes or gene patterns. These codes or patterns, preserved in the dried tissue of mummified bodies, could be copied and placed in fertilized egg cells.

" 'For example, once the genetic code of a great genius is determined, hundreds of thousands of his duplicates can be created for the world's benefit . . .'

"Carlson said he is confident that nucleic acid crystals necessary to identify the mummy's genetic code will be found. He noted that other proteins discovered in such tissue have made it possible for scientists to type the blood of Egyptians who have been dead for tens of centuries.

"Carlson said hundreds or thousands of a particular subject's body could be reconstituted.

" 'A cell pattern would be synthesized according to the gene pattern of the mummy, and then this synthetic nucleus would be surgically planted in a fertilized cell from which the original nucleus had been removed. . . .

" 'The cell would then be allowed to multiply naturally, and when there were say, 64, it would be put into a solution that would loosen the membrane that held the cells together.

" 'There would then be 64 new single identical cells from which to start the process all over again.

" 'As soon as you had the desired number of single cells of King Tut—or of musical or mathematical geniuses— the cells would be allowed to complete their development into children,' he explained.

"His remarks were made at UCLA . . . on the subject The Human Agenda."

Those familiar with the Edgar Cayce readings will remember the automatons or "things" which existed in prehistoric times when there was more scientifically controlled production than there is today. As to their status:

Q.4. Were the thought forms that were able to push themselves out of themselves, inhabited by souls, or were they of the animal kingdom?

A.4 That as created by that created, of the animal kingdom. That created by the Creator, with the soul.   364-7

We would assume from this that reconstructed geniuses

would not have souls and, therefore, would not have real initiative.

Spiritual element, the vitality, produces the motive forces of the entity, whether physical or spiritual. Spiritual forces being the life, the reproductive principle, the soul, the development principle.   900-17

The function of the automatons was clearly defined.

We find that in those periods, there was not a laboring for the sustenance of life (as in the present), but rather individuals . . . were served by automatons or THINGS, that were retained by individuals or groups to do the labors of a household, or to cultivate the fields or the like, or to perform the activities of artisans or the like.   1968-2

We note that even height was regulated for utility.

. . . In the matter of form, as we find, there were those as projections from that about the animal kingdom; for the thought bodies gradually took form, and the various combinations (as may be called) of the various forces that called or classified themselves as gods, or rulers over—whether herds, or fowls, or fishes, etc.—in part much in the form of the present day man . . . these took on many sizes as to stature, from that as may be called the midget to the giants—for there were giants in the earth in those days, men as tall as (what would be termed today) ten to twelve feet in stature, and in proportion—well proportioned throughout.   364-11

A later news article notes that such a program as the one envisioned by Professor Carlson might meet with opposition and tells of a more recent suggestion that scientists may first experiment with imposing human characteristics on animals.

The Virginian-Pilot Norfolk, Va., November 27, 1966:

London—"It may soon be possible to propagate people in much the same way as we now propagate roses—by taking the equivalent of cuttings.

135

"According to the Nobel Prize-winning geneticist, Prof. Joshua Lederberg, writing in the *Bulletin of the Atomic Scientists,* we should consider the implications of this now, since it would offer the possibility of making dozens or hundreds of genetically identical individuals like multiplied identical twins.

"Biologists are agreed that such techniques are likely to come; the main uncertainty is when? Lederberg suggests it is more likely to be in 'a few years rather than decades.'

"The essential features of the technique have already been demonstrated in frogs, the professor says, and may be achieved in higher animals any day. The procedure would be to take a nucleus from the cell of the individual it is desired to duplicate, and implant it into a human ovary cell, which would then be implanted in the womb to develop.

"The normal fertilized egg contains genetic material from both parents. But the cell nucleus from any tissue in an individual's body contains the complete genetic 'blueprint' belonging to him. Thus, by using this as a 'cutting' from which to propagate a new individual, an identical twin should result.

"If it worked for a man, it would be possible to freeze some tissues of, for example, an Einstein, and use the nuclei later to produce more Einsteins. Biologists 'would at least enjoy being able to observe . . . whether a second Einstein would outdo the first one,' says Lederberg. But there would be 'accompanying social friction.'

"The possibilities will raise in an acute form the question of what we understand by human identity and individuality, the professor says. Human 'clones'—as such a propagated strain of genetically identical people would be called—might be able to communicate with exceptional ease, as identical twins can. The military might be interested in this. Furthermore, being generally identical, tissues and organs could be transplanted from one to another without difficulty.

"On the other hand, the biological strength of man as a species is his variability and his adaptability, which allow him to meet all kinds of new circumstances.

"Clones could find themselves in an evolutionary rut,

suitable only for one particular specialized role. So clone propagation would have to be supplemented by conventional propagation, to maintain genetic variability. Plant breeders, the professor says, strike a similar balance between vegetative and sexual propagation.

"The cloning technique would be irresistible for breeders of race-horses and prize cattle, who in principle could duplicate a particular Derby winner indefinitely. But biological discoveries may lead into still stranger territory, Lederberg predicts. For it may become possible to incorporate part of a human nucleus into the germ cell of some animal, say a gorilla, which might produce various 'sub-human' hybrids.

"Indeed such experiments are likely to precede any effort to produce 'clone' humans, 'because of the touchiness of experimentation on obviously human material.' Such experiments will be 'pushed in steps as far as biology will allow,' to incorporate larger and larger proportions of human genetic material into animals, and perhaps also to incorporate tissues and organs.

" 'These are not the most congenial subjects for friendly conversation,' Lederberg concludes, 'especially if the conversants mistake comment for advocacy.' His main aim is to emphasize that the relevant biological advances may be made very soon.

"The techniques are likely to be tried 'even without an adequate basis of understanding of human values, not to mention vast gaps in human genetics.'

"This makes it essential to think out the implications beforehand, since otherwise policies are likely to be based on 'the accidents of the first advertised samples.'

"Public opinion might be determined by the nationality or public esteem of the cloned person, or 'the handsomeness of the parahuman progeny.'

"The prediction and modification of human nature, the professor urges, badly need the planning and 'informed foresight' which we apply to other aspects of life."

The Edgar Cayce readings have information on beings part-human, part-animal.

. . . in that particular experience there were still

137

those who were physically entangled in the animal kingdom with appendages, with cloven hoofs, with four legs, with portions of trees, with tails, with scales, with those various things that thought forms (or evil) had so indulged in as to separate the purpose of God's creation of man, as man—not as animal but as man. And the animal seeks only gratifying of self, the preservation of life, the satisfying of appetites. With infinity injected in same brought the many confused activities or thoughts that we know now as appetites. Yes, a dog may learn to smoke! Yes, a horse may learn to eat sugar! But these are not natural inclinations—rather man's influence upon these activities by associations.   2072-8

These hybrid beings are clearly pictured by the early Egyptians, Assyrians, Greeks, Mayans, Incas, (Asian) Indians, Javanese and Easter Islanders, either in sculptured or pictorial representations or in stories which we have classed as mythology because among other things we could not bring ourselves to accept the existence of such oddities.

Eventually in ancient Egypt, according to the Edgar Cayce readings, a program was undertaken in which individuals were able to lose these appendages.

There were many periods or days required for the building up of the body, as represented by the group that acted in the capacity of the active individuals about the building of these edifices or temples that were to represent then the recreation (re-creation) halls . . . there were the preparations for the spiritual worship that comprised not only the sacrificial altars, which were not as for the offering of sacrifice in the slaying of animal or bird, or beast, or reptile, or man; rather that upon which individuals put their faults and blotted them out with the fires of those forces that were set in motion.   294-148

Reference to the use of power from crystals which resemble the lasers and masers of today.

. . . the bodies were changing in their forms as

138

their developments or purifications were effective in those temples, where the consecrations and changes were taking place by the activities of the individuals in their abilities to turn themselves towards (in the mental) the spiritual things of an existence. They gradually lost, then, many feathers from their legs. Many of them lost hairs from the body, that were gradually taken away. Many gradually began to lose their tails, or their protuberances in their various forms. Many of them gradually lost those forms of the hand and foot, as they were changed from claws—or paws—to those that might be more symmetrical with the body. Hence the activities or the uses of the body, as they became more erect and more active, more shaped to their various activities.   294-149

And with these expressions there were those who chose the activities that were set in motion for the purifying of their bodies, that there might be the purifrying of physical conditions which had been and were being effected by the emotional forces, or the carnal influences about them in the experience. Such activities might be best expressed or explained by comparing same to the present hospitalizations; where there might be operative measures used for the removal of such as tumors, breaks, growths or the like ... Rather he that would be justified is much as were those who purified their bodies from appendages, such as tails, feathers, wings, and portions of the natural sources.   281-43

The cycle seems to have come full round.
We agree with Professor Lederberg that "the implications" of a clone program should be thought out "beforehand" and, we add—in the light of the Edgar Cayce readings—*very thoroughly*.

TELEPATHY

from the Edgar Cayce Readings

Since telepathy is often mentioned as one example of ESP, it is interesting to note that Edgar Cayce was asked about this phenomenon on May 6, 1937. The question put to him in his trance state explained that a group of individuals had been attempting elementary experiments in both telepathy and card guessing in connection with the general work of the Association for Research and Enlightenment. The desire was expressed to make those experiments of practical value, thus to add to the general knowledge of the laws of telepathy and simple clairvoyance, and the question asked for advice as to the proper procedure. This is the answer given:

In the study of the phenomena of this nature, there should be first the questions and answers—or the analysis as to purpose—not only in the minds of those who would lend themselves in such an experience but in the minds of those who would lend themselves in such experiments as a part of the research work of such an organization as the Association for Research and Enlightenment. As in this manner:

What is expected? What is the *source* of the information as may be had in such experiments, that goes beyond that called or termed the ordinary mind guessing? Or what is the basis of telepathic or clairvoyant communication? Or what are these in their elemental activity, or in all activity?

To be sure, the experience is a portion of the Mind; but Mind, as we have given, is both material *and* spiritual.

Now: From what order, or from what basis then, is such information sought by those who join in such experiments?

140

It is the basis of all relationship of the individual entity—the cosmic or the universal forces. Or, to make it simple—yet most complex: "Know—the Lord thy God is ONE!" KNOW the Lord thy God is ONE!

Then the communications or the abilities for the activity of the Mind of an entity in such an experiment are *not* because of, or from, an association of entities.

It is not then to be presumed, supposed, or proposed, to be a calling upon, a depending upon, a seeking for, that which is without—or that outside of self; but rather the attuning of self to the divine within, which is (the divine) a universal or *the* universal consciousness.

This is proposed then as the basis for such investigation, and those who accredit or seek or desire other sources—Well, keep their records separate, and the more oft they will be found to be such as those that are patterns or examples in Holy Writ; namely, an excellent one, Saul, the first king. Here we find an example of an individual seeking from the man of God, or the prophet, information to be given clairvoyantly, telepathically (if you choose to use such terms); and we find the incident used as an illustration that may be well kept to the forefront in the minds of those who would prompt or check or record such experiments.

As to making practical application; it is what you do with the abilities that are developed by this attunement in coordinating, cooperating one with another in such experiments.

There are those in the group who have experimented that are gifted; gifted meaning then *innately* developed by the use of those faculties of the mind to attune themselves to the Infinite.

Also there are those who have attuned themselves to a consciousness *not* wholly within themselves, but *prompted* by those who would become prompters—as in *any* attunement that is ever attempted in material consciousness, it is subject to same.

Then there is to be the proper consideration, or

141

the proper evaluation of that which is gained by the experience of each that joins in with same.

This may be set as a criterion to any—yes, to all: When such an experiment, such a trial, draws or tires, or makes the mind foggy or dull or becomes as a drain upon the physical energies, know you are attuning wrong—and static has entered, from *some* source!

Ready for questions.

Q-1. Please suggest the type of experiments which may be conducted most successfully by this group.

A-1. Well, you would have to take each as an individual—to say as to which may be the most successful! For there are grades, there are variations. There are in the group, as has been indicated, curiosity, wisdom, folly, *and* those things that make for real spiritual development. They each then require first—FIRST—self-analysis! WHAT prompts the individual to seek, engage, or desire to join in such experiments? As to how far, as to what—there is no end! Is there any end to infinity? For this is the attunement, then—to Infinity!

Each will find a variation according to the application and the abilities of each to become less and less controlled by personality, and the more and more able to shut away the material consciousness—or the mind portion that is of the material, propagated or implied by what is termed the five senses. The more and more each is impelled by that which is intuitive, or the relying upon the soul force within, the greater, the farther, the deeper, the broader, the more constructive may be the result.

More and more, then, turn to those experiments that are not only helpful but that give hope to others, that make for the activity of the fruits of the Spirit.

Make haste slowly.

Wait on the *Lord;* not making for a show, an activity of any kind that would be self-glorification, self-exaltation, but rather that which is helpful, hopeful for others.   792-2

142

Thus, we see, when discussing telepathy as well as all the other expressions of extrasensory perception, the Edgar Cayce readings emphasize the same points over and over. First, self-examination as to the true purpose; second, realization of the necessity of turning to the divine within, or the universal consciousness. The stress was always that the universal consciousness is constructive, not destructive.

The following answers were given to people who were interested in developing their psychic abilities.

Q-2. Would it be wise for me to develop what psychic abilities I seem to have now, so that these would be under control and called upon at will for aid to others?

A-2. Be decidedly well. For, the body, the mind, is well fitted as a channel; so that, by entering into meditation there may come those influences from its own abilities as a seeress, as a prophetess, as a high priestess in that experience, to know the needs of the individuals as they seek.

Credit the power to the divine as it manifests through self. For it is that self-expression that is needed in the preparation and in the ministering of same as to the needs of others.

Q-3. Will this develop normally and naturally, or should there be a deliberate attempt?

A-3. As it were, expose self to its development; not by force but by entering into meditation—allowing the influence of the generative force through the glandular system to be raised to the various centers; first for the purifying of self, then for the obtaining of that necessary—through symbol, sign or vision—to be accomplished for individuals seeking.

Q-3. Is there any evidence that I have, or could develop, supernormal powers?

A-4. This depends upon the qualifications, or as to what is termed supernormal powers. There is within every soul the ability to accomplish any influence that has been or may be accomplished in

143

the earth. If the development of the psychic abilities is meant here, these might be developed, dependent upon what the entity seeks as its ideal or as his guide. There is *one* way, but there are many paths.

Q-4. *Do I have healing ability?*

A-4. This may be developed. The power, as does all good, must come from the one source. Then live thine own life in such a way and manner as to merit the use of such power; not to thine own glory, but to the glory of the Giver of all good and perfect gifts.

3083-1

CAST OUT FEAR

Roland Klemm

Fear is the negation of the Spirit of God—the life—within us. And life is the expression of love, of the working of God's creative power within and through us toward the rest of his creation.

. . . As has been so often quoted and so little interpreted in people's lives, the consciousness of God's presence, as manifested in Christ, casteth out fear.

3691-1

At least having looked at fear squarely, and having achieved an intellectual grasp and understanding, we need no longer "fear the fear." To paraphrase: Once we become conscious of what we are doing, we shall no longer need to avoid many areas of life's expression. We shall be able to live God's life joyfully and enthusiastically as He intended!

Fear takes many forms, and walks in many guises. In its simplest forms, we know it as the vague feelings of discomfort and uneasiness that we refer to as "worry" and "anxiety." We somehow impute an unfortunate outcome of *something* to *some indeterminate time* in the future—with our*selves* being the star participants and recipients of these nameless woes. Were we honestly to face ourselves, and to tabulate all the times these "things" did *not* materialize, against all the times they actually *did*, no one would be more surprised at the comical imbalance presented than we!

However, this is not the point. We do have these unpleasant and unhappy feelings, and would for all the world that something would happen to get us out of our moroseness. Let us see how this comes about. We shall then be in a better position to know how to deal effectively with the situations as they arise, day by day.

We believe that, basic to all forms of fear, is the impression of being helpless and alone—of being weak and unable to cope with whatever situations God, and life, send our way. There is a feeling of incompleteness in being away from our Creator, and this is often reflected on earth in our attitudes of seeming "lost" away from parents and loved ones—who, in a certain limited sense, are surrogates for the perfect love we left behind.

More broadly, Mr. Cayce's readings indicate a good many more concrete sources of fear—sources that the modern Western scientific world has yet to discover.

We read of astrological influences, which, it is pointed out, tend to cause fears to arise in the entity under consideration. We read of these emotions on occasion as being residuals of past lives; of being due to "far memory." In turn, these are somehow reinforced and intertwined with the realistic, present-day unpleasant relationships we all experience.

In [5424-1] the reading tells of a past life when the entity was companion to Queen Anne of England:

While under those troublesome periods these brought many of those doubts and fears we find in the present: "What will people say?" What will be the ultimate outcome of the environmental forces of those who may be yielded to, won, or guided by, influences of the entity?

We might call this a "fear of the unknown, relative to other people."

145

In that experience [a past life] many varied feelings toward individuals, toward groups, became a part of the experience, and the presence of doubts and fears of men, and doubts and fears of women, are parts of the consciousness of the entity. 5725-1

The reading adds, "In sacred or in classical music may the entity find relief."

We find a further, more subtle relationship in this reading:

The entity lost, in this experience, through fear, created in self by misuse, misleading [others] when the truth was known innately. Fear hinders. 105-2

On the other tack:

In the astrological aspects we find the entity is one with a great deal of strength of character, strength of purpose; and yet so easily persuaded or dissuaded by material circumstances—yet innately knowing there is a way that seemeth right unto a man though the end thereof is death, is disappointment, is that which maketh the heart afraid. 1849-2

Evidently we do have a portion of our consciousness which is relatively inaccessible to most of us, but which somehow has registered our sins and misdeeds of the past, and even today continually brings us face to face with situations which we will have to meet—and conquer—at one time or another. But more of this later.

To backtrack momentarily to the more practical aspects of everyday living, fears come under many headings familiar to us all. There are specific fears—of noise, of closed places, of falling, of the phenomena of life, of material conditions. There are social fears—of being left alone, of what others may say, of censure, of people generally. There are indeterminate fears—of the future, of advancing age, of death, and of the "world beyond." We can learn to read them and to understand them.

More important, it seems, are the fears a person has of

himself and, apparently, of his ability to control his own feelings in the here and now.

It is self-consciousness that brings fear.   3357-2

In thine own heart come those things that would make afraid. But fear is of the earth. The Spirit of Truth and Righteousness casteth out fear.   397-1

Selfishness is what makes men afraid . . . Fear is cast aside by wholly relying upon His promise, that one may demand to be fulfilled. "The Father knoweth what ye have need of before ye have asked." Peace is with thee, contentment is in thy hand, who becomes not afraid but trusts rather in Him.   262-29

Fear in self and of self's abilities present themselves to be overcome . . . through hardship . . . (relating to work, position, business relationships.)   39-8

And here we begin to see the function of fear as building character.

We do also have a very real part to play in our own growth and destiny. In one situation or another, we attract to ourselves that which we will have to face—the lack of self-confidence, the feeling of inferiority. [4082-1] indicates that the causes of so much fear in the entity's life were that the entity lacked sincerity, lacked the coordination in carrying its ideals and purposes into practice in former lives on earth as well as in the present one. The entity's inferiority complex originated "From the fear or dislike of men."

In [87-1], after enumeration of physical deficiencies, ". . . patient is afraid of himself; in other words, does not have self-confidence."

One other aspect bears mention here—that of not relinquishing responsibility for one's own actions as befits an adult.

The entity is oft prone to give power to influences

without self. This causes much of the [entity's] fear. 5030-1

These influences without self also include other people, whom we sometimes allow to run our lives in a manner we know to be to our detriment, rather than risk an unpleasant scene. Here we have a psychological conflict, in that standing up to them may mean (in the depths of our consciousness) having the fear of losing that particular loved one. Classically, it is known as a double approach-avoidance conflict and has the unhappy result of really keeping us in a bind. We fume and fret, and become ever more constricted and fearful, since we are unaware of the part our own inner reactions have played.

To summarize: "Fear is the greatest destructive force to man's intelligence [101-1]," and unfits the body to meet the needs of the hour [39-4, slightly paraphrased].

The biological relationships can perhaps best be understood with a brief, if overly general, review of the interrelatedness of the central nervous system and the peripheral, or autonomic, nervous system. Both, when operating smoothly and in unison, serve their own specific functions of coordinating man's activities.

The central nervous system (CNS)—brain, spinal cord, sensory and motor nerve networks—can be thought of as the active, controlling and integrating system. Psychologically, it represents the will, volition, and controlled interaction with the environment.

The autonomic nervous system can be thought of as the automatic regulating system of the vegetative functions of the body—heart, blood pressure, digestion, excretion (including perspiration and respiration), chemical balance, etc. It is further subdivided into two fairly distinct systems—the sympathetic, and the parasympathetic. The sympathetic is essentially expansive or facilitating of emotional behavior; the parasympathetic, constrictive.

Furthermore, the autonomic nervous system is under fairly direct and rapid control of the central nervous system. One need only observe the rapid blanching of the face when a person becomes angry, or the crimson blush

148

that spreads quickly with social embarrassment, to appreciate something of the speed with which this reaction takes place.

The relatedness is not a one way street however, since changes induced in the autonomic nervous system through the intermediary of the CNS, reflect back upon the CNS over a longer period of time in the form of chemical imbalances, constriction of the local blood supply to glands, nerves, digestive organs, muscle groups, areas of the brain, etc. It can easily be appreciated that this will have the long-term effect of molding the personality and temperament of an individual.

One can eat plenty of good food, for instance, but if the stomach is blanched and knotted with rage (literally), the digestive secretions will not be produced and the potential nutrients in the food will not be released to be assimilated into the blood stream to feed other parts of the system which need it. The entire system suffers.

Here it becomes part of the function of the "self," acting through the central coordinating system, to set things right, as it were, and once again to bring about the proper balance. Excerpts from readings later on will illustrate this nicely.

A few illustrations follow, which will give the reader a more comprehensive understanding of the opposing attitudes generated by "faith" and "fear," as reflected in the functioning of the autonomic nervous system.

These should give the reader a basis against which to project the data given in the readings on the following pages, and are taken from a little-known book, *The Physiology of Faith and Fear*, by William S. Sadler, M.D.

In the sensory modalities, taste, smell, hearing, and sight; faith increases, sharpens, renders more acute, and generally enhances. Sensations and temperatures are normal; the feelings more acute. Speech is more fluent. The expression becomes youthful and healthful, with the glow of nutritious blood right at the surface; the countenance is happy, courageous, optimistic, and joyful.

With fear dominant, the opposite holds true. Taste is blunted or abolished; smell is decreased, abolished, or distorted; hearing is affected adversely; sight is distorted, or mis-registers as delusions and/or "hysterical blindness." Feeling sensations are rendered unreliable, and the temperature sensation false. Speech may be strained or paralyzed, or erratic stuttering can occur. The expression is usually morbid and unhappy, the countenance downcast and despondent.

As to the general physiological functioning when faith is present—the complexion is ruddy, and pulse regular, slow, and strong. Circulation is normal and warm. The local blood supply is regular and even, with movement accelerated. Hands and feet are warm. Capillary contraction is normal, with elimination increased.

All this is reflected grossly as an elastic gait, an erect and vigorous carriage, a relaxed and agreeable expression, and increased work capacity.

With fear dominant, the complexion becomes pale and anemic; the pulse weak, irregular, and rapid. Circulatory equilibrium favors edema and local stagnation, and is poor and chilly. Capillary contraction is spasmodic and irregular. Perspiration is checked, elimination decreased. The gait becomes dragging and slovenly, the carriage stooped and weak. Expression is downcast and sorrowful, and the work capacity is markedly decreased.

To summarize: the attitude of faith reflects all the positive aspects of a vigorous, outgoing expression of life lived fully and at peace with the Creator, while fear is indicative of its opposite.

Back, once more, to the readings, we find a continual admonition to *change the attitude* by an act of will. When we change the attitude over so long a period of time that it becomes habitual, we cannot help but reflect *that* Life, *that* Love, within whose bounds we were intended to exist. Similarly, we cannot help but convey this love of God toward others—if merely by radiating warmth, strength, and vitality!

In considering the next section, we run the gamut from some quite specific conditions to the more generalized and comprehensive outlines both of inter-relationships within the body itself, and between the felt attitudes and resultant conditions. We have here a great deal of food for thought. Basically, the self does the moving—initiates the activity—somewhat analogous to the way "God Moved" and initiated His Creation. And in initiating a change, the conditions are not quite what they were beforehand. All we need see is that the activity is in the right direction—toward God.

One of the greatest hindrances to the body is fear. Not of others; not of mental ability; not of that which the body desires, but fear in the physical innate forces of the body. And while often one's outlook upon life is altered by the conditions of the liver or of the digestive system, in this particular body, while these conditions exist, fear produces almost as much harmful effect as this particular physical condition.

While there may be applied that for the body that will overcome physically those deficiencies, yet unless that basic force as is present in the fear of the body is removed, these physical deficiencies would certainly return to hinder the body again. In casting out same, replace grudge, hatred, and kindred conditions (products of fear) with the love of the Master.   (5735-1)

In the physical forces, or through these channels, there have been builded fears, disappointments, and related things, bringing to the body those ills incident to such conditions. This, in its final analysis, is due to lack of faith, hope, and the inability of the body to do *with pleasure* those things it finds hard to do.

Q.   What can the body do to take away fear?
A.   This may only be taken away by losing it in His power, His might, through spiritual and mental concentration upon the self being a channel of the Creator.   5470-1

We find there are disturbances, but these are more from fear internally than from any specific causes physically . . . Then cast out fear. That is, know the spiritual forces in which you believe. Apply them in thy relationships to thy fellow men.   3534-1

Q.   Why has the patient a fear of the future? Why does he not want to live?
A.   The natural tendency of the gnawing from

151

within, and the pressure created in the upper portion of the system from same, distorts the view of the body as well as those depressions from the associations about same, but with a changed physical outlook the whole outlook of the body, mentally and physically, will also be changed. 5437-1

There are abilities in abundance in the entity for activities if they are put into use from the seed of the Spirit of Truth, and not from those of hate, malice, jealousy, and the things that make people afraid, the things that cause timidity within the associations, and fear.

For as has been so often quoted and so little interpreted in people's lives, the consciousness of God's presence, as manifested in Christ, casteth out fear.

3691-1

We find there are conditions of which the body should take cognizance. Yet if there is held in the mental self a fear, there will come those conditions that are spoken of by the psalmist, "That which I feared hath come upon me." Then apply in nature that which will meet the needs for eliminating the infection that may have been carried in the circulation from those disturbances that have existed. This will in the physical self eliminate the sources, if the fear is eliminated from the mental self that blocks such activity in the living organism in the body. 2650-1

(Reading then prescribes treatment.)

The readings point out again and again that fear aggravates bodily ills and prevents their healing.

An admonition to one whose ailment could not be treated directly:

Study very closely those activities of His chosen people as they were prepared to enter the Promised Land, and yet from doubt, from fear, were rejected. Be not among those that would be rejected. 3461-1

Q. *What is causing the intense pain in the upper back?*

A. General nerve reactions in the body . . . fear. ·3658-1

Diagnosis of a difficult and distressing case ends thus: This, as we find, is *not* a brain lesion, but a *fearfulness* in the soul of the entity. 3114-1

The tautness in the cerebro-spinal comes from the fear as is from within, and this acting upon the ganglia of the sympathetic and cerebro-spinal system often changes the reactions of the physical organs themselves. Not as wrath; not as of malice, but rather that of fear does the reaction show in the system. 5437-1

Fear, the greatest bugaboo to the human elements; for in fear come those conditions that destroy the vitality of that assimilated. To overcome fear, so fill the mental forces with that of a creative nature as to cast out fear; for he, or she, that is without fear is free indeed. 5439-1

Here indeed is food for thoughtful contemplation: quite extreme aches and pains can be due to localized turmoil based on fear, and unrecognized (or, more accurately, *unacknowledged*) anger and malice masquerading as something else!

But to get on with our story. Now that we begin to glimpse the hows and whys, what are we to do with this information? The readings have discussed some specific fears, and have suggested remedies.

First, we are to replace fear with love: we are to turn it into its opposite; we are to lose our concern for self in the service of others; we can sometimes see the humor in the situation and laugh instead of fret. ⁓

We can learn from it—regard it as an opportunity to develop our souls.

We can learn more perfectly to turn toward the light; to pray; to walk in His way; to place more trust in Him.

We can actively hold His light before us; do our duty as

it is presented; express our love through creative activity; become more subtly conscious of His abiding presence.

We can learn to exercise our wills in His service, and break the pattern of ill will, ill health, and half-living once and for all.

> Fear begetteth that that makes afraid; through fear man wanders far afield.
>
> 5502-3

> Replace fear ever with love.
>
> 3051-2

> Let fear, let worry, be lost in service to others for His Name's Sake.
>
> 281-61

> Use much of the experiences of others; speak out. Don't fear. Call on those near and hear what they have to say.
>
> 39-5

Psychologically, this is a good way to overcome uneasiness with people—to listen to them, and pay them the courtesy of acknowledging their existence and the worthwhileness of their thoughts. Eventually this attitude cannot help but be reflected back to oneself, and is a good way to help overcome the fear of being censured by others. Other specific fears will also tend to be ameliorated.

> *Q. How may I get rid of fear of closed places?*
> A. The attitude must be kept as to helpfulness in spiritual forces of the body—within and without.
>
> 5397-1

> *Q. How can I overcome fear of advancing old age and being alone?*
> A. By going out and doing something for somebody else; that is, those not able to do for themselves; making others happy, forgetting self entirely. These are as material manifestations, but in helping someone else you'll get rid of your feelings. 5226-1

Helpfulness to others is one way: a turning toward the

Light and active engagement in the problems of the day are other ways.

Shadows and doubts and fears will arise in thy experience, but keep before thee the light of all good consciousness, of all good and perfect service to Him, and ye will find that the shadows of fear will fall far behind.

Let those things that cause fears be far removed from thee, through just the little kindness, the little service ye may do here and there. For remember, these are at war with one another—hope and fear. Let not thy mind, let not thy body, let not thy purpose, thy desire entertain fear.   262-12

He that walketh in the shadow shall be afraid. Walk rather in the light of Creative forces, of Truth and ye shall not be afraid.   2021-12

For as is understood, He hath not willed that any should perish; yet because there are disturbances of the physical, material or mental nature . . . fears arise. These beget those influences that prevent the proper attunement.

Q. How may I overcome the innate fear which prevents attunement with the Christ?

A. Let that which causes fear be taken up [dissolved] in the willingness, the desire, to be of help to others.   69-4

Q. (paraphrase) Is it not a proper purpose that [254] be supplied with sufficient and abundant material substance to free him from the necessity to overwork in order to provide a living?

A. Remember, my children, it is the fear of the material conditions that wrecks the material body. It is the *fear* of this or that, that prevents a channel from making for the greater supply.   254-85

There may be fear created by the mental body becoming so absorbed in physical disturbances or so absorbing in things of self as to become fearful of all other things outside of itself.

Q. Why am I so frightened and apprehensive all the time, so that I fear company and yet fear to be alone?
A. The anxieties should be controlled . . . by defining, or confining self to some particular form of ideal, and following through with that . . . Apply self to the ideal presentation of what spirit, mental body and physical body represent in the world as found in the 30th chapter of Deuteronomy and the 14th, 15th, 16th, and 17th chapters of John's Gospel.   1776-1

Q. How can I overcome fears that beset me, especially about myself and my wife?
A. Fear is the root of most of the ills of mankind whether of self, or of what others think of self, or how self will appear to others. To overcome fear is to fill the mental, spiritual being with that which wholly casts out fear: the love manifest in the world through Him who gave Himself a ransom for many. Such love, such understanding casts out fear. Be ye not fearful; that thou sowest, that thou must reap. Be more mindful of that sown.   5459-3

Q. What is the cause of my fear?
A. Self-condemnation.

Q. How may I overcome it?
A. By seeing the ridiculous, the funny side of every experience. Knowing and believing in whom ye have trusted, in the Lord: for without that consciousness of the indwelling Spirit little may ever be accomplished.   5302-1
The forces and the fears of phenomena of life often times prevent the entity from accomplishing most, by the fear of what others will say. Put this aside.   13-1

Q. Career as a pianist was brought to an end through my extreme nervousness and lack of con-
156

fidence, and other talents have suffered because of an overpowering fear. What am I to do?

A. . . . Right about face! Know it is within thee! Defying this has brought the fear, has brought the anxieties. Turn about, and pray a little oftener. Do this several weeks, yes—let a whole moon pass, or a period of a moon—28 days—and never fail to pray at two o'clock in the morning. Rise and pray—facing east! Ye will be surprised at how much peace and harmony will come into thy soul.   3509-1

There are at least two unusual readings whch should be mentioned, and although they hardly fall within our general framework, they do indicate some unusual aspects of fears—showing that some fears *are rightly placed,* even though we are not cognizant of the real causes.

One indicates a residue of a past life acting quite strongly.

Q. How can I overcome the social fear which causes me to shun leadership?

A. This is well for the entity, and this ye overcame in the experience before this. Keep it as it is. Don't be a social climber. *Don't* depend on social activities. Be a home builder. Do *not* attempt to make a life outside the home.   3474-1

The other reading was for a patient frantic because her mind seemed in disorder. She suffered from a feeling of losing her grip, inability to concentrate, lapse of memory, and dizziness. This gave rise to fears. The reading said that anxiety was the cause of some of these mental aberrations, but added:

Fear not . . . it is evidently the *psychic* attempting to come through . . . If there is set a definite period or manner of meditation . . . there may be had a balancing . . . Let thy mind, thy body be consecrated to the Lord to have His way with thee . . .

Each day *purify* the body, the mind, as ye enter into that period of communication in prayer, in supplication. He will give thee understanding; He will

157

give thee wisdom as to how ye shall conduct thy-
self day by day.   1089-2

Surround yourself with the consciousness of a walk and
talk with Him: a period of quiet; a trust in the Lord; a
place where your Spirit can bear witness with His.

Fear God, and keep His commandments; for this is the
whole duty of man. (Eccl. 12:13)

CLUES TO THE MYSTERY OF EGYPT

Violet M. Shelley

The unusual legacy of psychically obtained information
left by the late Edgar Cayce offers innumerable avenues
for research, but among the most fascinating are those
which have no sign posts from historians, no clearly
defined maps. The great mystery of Egypt, which has
teased men's minds for centuries, finds a possible solution
in these readings; yet research into their validity must go
on, and we look to Egyptological evidence for further
clues. Perhaps eventually these clues will lead to final
proof.

Very briefly, the Edgar Cayce data postulated that a
leader, Arart, from the Caucasian area, went into Egypt
with his people and conquered it around 10,500 B.C.
They indicated that his rule had centered around Gizeh
and that the monuments there were built in part during the
rule of his son Araaraart. With Arart had come a priest,
Ra-ta, who attempted to organize religious practices and
bring the people to the idea of the One Creative Principle,
and the continuity of life.

Wallis Budge, whose works on both the religion and the
antiquities of Egypt have done so much toward the
world's understanding, has written that interpreters of
Egyptian religion fall into two classes. The first class, he
says, are those who regard that religion as a product of

158

half-savage men, and who think it but a mixture of crude nature cults and superstition. The second class are those who think they are able to trace a steady development in the religion until it reached a point at which it possessed highly evolved concepts about God and man's relationship to Him.

Students of the Edgar Cayce readings have come to think that there is a third way to look at Egyptian religious beliefs: as a corruption of the tenets of the Law of One God. They see in the pantheon of Egyptian gods and goddesses personifications of the Deific attributes, an attempt to make abstract ideas concrete.

James Henry Breasted in his book, *The Dawn of Conscience,* says that the Egyptians had possessed a standard of morals far superior to that of the Decalogue—and had them well over a thousand years before the Decalogue appeared. He very emphatically believes that our moral heritage derives from a wider human past, enormously older than the Hebrews. He claims that our moral heritage came to us *through* the Hebrews rather than *from* them.

Many scholars have made a point of comparing stelae texts of philosophical and religious inspiration with certain of our Proverbs and Psalms. They find them astonishingly similar in both ideas and mode of expression. Such scholarly implications suggest to many that the religion of Egypt as known in history is in fact a corruption rather than an evolvement. Perhaps, in fact, in the mists of prehistory there was such a priest as the readings mentioned—a priest who taught the Law of One God.

In 1939, a reading indicated that such a priest and religious group did come to Egypt, from an Eastern source.

. . . The Priest was an individual who had received inspiration from within. And, realizing that such an influence or force might be given to others in their search for WHY and WHAT were their purposes in material life, he then sought out one who might foster such a study in materiality. Thus, from those places that were a portion of what is now called the Carpathias, he came with a great horde, or a great number (as to individual souls, numbering nine hundred), into the land now called Egypt . . .   281-42

. . . The entity then occupying that position as the counselor to the ruler Arart at that time, coming as he did from the plains country of now the Arabian to the rule of the Egyptian forces as were first set in Gizeh . . .   953-13

What evidence for such an Eastern source is there among present day historians? Samuel Mercer in Volume IV of *The Pyramid Texts* refers to the possible north-eastern origin of Re and his followers. He says that perhaps they came from the Caucasus. He suggests that the characteristics of these leader gods indicate that they were more intellectually and culturally advanced people who had settled in the apex of the Delta. In October 1934, a report by Petrie in the *Literary Digest* concerned itself with evidence of repeated invasions into Egypt from the Caucasian area which had started in the Badarian age, near the beginning of Egypt's history.

The Edgar Cayce readings, in describing the physical appearance of these invading people, mention many times fair hair (or red hair) and blue or gray eyes—hardly the history book concept of swarthy skin and dark sloe-eyes! Reading #275-39 has within it the description of six different characters, all of whom were fair haired, with light eyes.

Are there indeed any clues in the Egyptological evidence to bear this out? In fact, in the Old Kingdom *mastaba* tomb of Princess Mersoankh between the Great Pyramid and the Sphinx at Gizeh there is a wall painting of a woman with yellow hair. The hair color has long been a puzzle. Scholars have asked, "Is it a wig, or is the natural hair color?" If it is the latter, it is the first evidence of such.

In the Cairo Museum in the Old Kingdom section there is a small wooden statue with painted blue eyes. There are also some statues which have inset eyes of crystal—some blue-gray, some brown in color. There are four unusual spare heads (considered to be portraits of the four sons of Chephren) which have Caucasian features and profiles. It is interesting to note, when considering physical appearance, that in the wall paintings, women were customarily painted with light yellow skin and men with reddish-brown skin. One theory is that the men were tanned from their work outdoors.

The Cayce readings pictured a different type of dress for the prehistoric Egyptians from that shown in most places.

> . . . [the entity] was robed in the garments of the Temple itself, in what later became the character of Egyptian robes of that particular period, made from the linens of the papyrus and the lotus combined and covered with the combination of the colors—purple and white—used as the robes of those so offering themselves . . .
>
> 276-6

> . . . The robes of the priest would be blue-gray, with the hooded portion back from the head, while about the waist would be a cord of gold color, with a purple tassel—or one of the tassels showing. The sandals would be of papyrus or woven grass . . .
>
> 585-10

A small wooden statue in the Cairo Museum, and a large limestone statue from Gizeh, Fourth Dynasty, are represented as wearing what is described as unusual dress—a type of robe rather than the kilt the Egyptians usually wore in the Old Kingdom period.

As one studies the available histories, one realizes that Egypt never had a genuine historian, and that the absence of a continuous sense of time made exact evaluation difficult. Each new king mounted the throne in the year *One;* when he died, the year *One* of his successor began the day of accession to the throne. Exact computation of past centuries was almost impossible.

Imprecision of dates and priestly preoccupation with the annalistic and royal lists weighed down for more than thirty centuries the notions of historical facts in Egypt. Yet the Cayce readings take history beyond even this point, and in readings given as early as 1925 mention a predynastic period. Space does not permit citing all the examples.

161

Q.1. What was the date, as man knows time, of this battle? (when Arart came into Egypt.)

A.1. Ten thousand and fifty-six years before the Prince of Peace came . . . 900-275

. . . and this ruler, Araaraart, being then the second of the Northern kings, and followed in the rule of the father, Arart, and began the rule, or took the position as the leader in his sixteenth year . . .

Q.2. Was this entity, as history gives it, one of the Pharaohs, or Rameses?

A.2. As one of the Pharaohs, of which there were more than three thousand. 341-9

James Breasted in his *Annals of Dynastic Kings* says that the Palermo Stone is an incomplete fragment containing annals from predynastic times to the middle of the Fifth Dynasty. The kings represented just prior to the dynastic kings are shown with a single crown (either of Upper or Lower Egypt). A fragment found later which fits this shows kings with the double crown of Upper and Lower Egypt, but the names are missing. This would seem to indicate a predynastic union before the separation into two kingdoms and the consequent dynastic union effected by Menes around 3500 B.C.

Howard Vyse, in Volume II of *Pyramids of Gizeh,* has a section on Arab historians' versions of the pyramids. Three of these versions indicate that the two pyramids were antediluvian.

There is also scholarly evidence which suggests Edgar Cayce's description of people who were leader gods. Such evidence can be found in Samuel Mercer's *The Pyramid Texts,* in Volumes I and IV—which speak of gods as historical figures. On the back wall of the Osiris chapel in the Temple of Seti I at Abydos, the gods are represented as living people without the divine headdress.

When speaking of hieroglyphics, the Edgar Cayce readings said, in 1934:

. . . In those periods the entity persuaded many of those to make for the activities that would preserve to the people what would be in the present termed

162

recipes or placards and drawings, and the like, that were the first of such intents brought to the Egyptian peoples (to be sure, not to the Atlanteans, but to the natives and those who had joined there to preserve such records) and the first attempt to make for a *written* language.   516-2

. . . With the periods of reconstruction after the return of the Priest, the entity joined with those who were active in putting the records in forms that were partially of the old characters of the ancient or early Egyptian, and part in the newer form of the Atlanteans. These may be found, especially when the house or tomb of records is opened, in a few years from now . . .   2537-1

In 1952, *The American Journal of Archeology* reported that in the West Cemetery of the Great Pyramid, in the large, stone *Mastaba* of Persen, there is a subsidiary tomb with unusual hieroglyphs and rare word forms carved on the doors. Vyse, in *Pyramids of Gizeh*, tells of hieroglyphic marks difficult to decipher, in the upper relieving chamber above the King's chamber in the Great Pyramid.

James Breasted, in *A History of Egypt,* says, "The hieroglyphs for the Northern Kingdom, for its king, and for its treasury can not have arisen at one stroke with the first king of the dynastic age; but must have been in use long before the rise of the First Dynasty; while the presence of a cursive linear hand at the beginning of the dynasties is conclusive evidence that the system was not then a recent innovation." In the First Dynasty, 3400 B.C. there was reference to *two* forms of writing—the hieroglyphic and the cursive.

The tomb of King Araaraart, alluded to in so many of the Cayce readings, has not been discovered. Yet, Egyptologists tell us that large archaic *mastaba* tombs have been found between the Sphinx and the Nile—one such being at Khafra Batraan. Those found were empty, but their size suggests the possibility of multiple burials of a king and his family.

The riddle of the Sphinx gains more of the embroidery of intrigue in the Cayce readings which speak of vaults at its base and a Hall of Records. Here the Cayce readings are not alone, for tradition has had it that there are secret passageways under the Sphinx.

Q.6. In what capacity did this entity act regarding the building of the Sphinx?
A.6. As the monuments were being rebuilt in the plains of that now called the Pyramid of Gizeh, this entity builded, laid, the foundations; that is, superintended same, figured out the geometrical position of same as [in?] relation to those buildings as were put up of that connecting the Sphinx, and the data concerning same may be found in the vaults in the base of the Sphinx. The entity with that dynasty, also in the second dynasty of Araaraart, when these buildings [were] begun. This laid out, base of Sphinx, in channels, and in the corner facing the Gizeh may be found that of the wording of how this was founded, giving the history of the first invading ruler and the ascension of Araaraart to that position.   195-15

. . . During this period was the completion of the memorial standing as the mystery of the ages today, and this, as is seen, represents this counselor to the kings, for, as is seen in the figure itself, not as one of the kings made in beast form, yet overseeing, supervising, giving counsel, giving strength, to the kings before and the kings since. The face, even as was given them is the representation of the counselor to this great people. These, and many findings, as given, may be found in the base of the left forearm, or leg, of the prostrate beast, in the base of foundation. Not in the underground *channel* (as was opened by the ruler many years, many centuries, later), but in the real base, or that as would be termed in the present parlance as the cornerstone . . .   953-24

Many readings mentioned "that monument or tomb or pyramid yet to be opened" which was the Hall of Records. Among the records to be found there eventually were to be the records "that were transferred from the destruction of the Atlantean land" (378-13). Information was requested as to the contents of the sealed room.

A record of Atlantis from the beginnings of those periods when the Spirit took form or began the encasements in that land, and the developments of the peoples throughout their sojourn, with the record of the first destruction and the changes that took place in the land, with the record of the *sojourning* of the peoples to the varied activities in other lands, and a record of the meetings of all the nations or lands for the activities in the destructions that became necessary, with the final destruction of Atlantis and the buildings of the pyramid of initiation, with who, what, where, would come the opening of the records that are as copies from the sunken Atlantis; for with the change it must rise again.

This in position lies, as the sun rises from the waters, the line of the shadow (or light) falls between the paws of the Sphinx, that was later set as the sentinel or guard, and which may not be entered from the connecting chambers from the Sphinx's paw (right paw) until the time has been fulilled when the changes must be active in this sphere of man's experience. Between, then, the Sphinx and the river.   378-16

Dr. Selim Hassan in Volume VII of *Excavations at Gizeh* acknowledges that Arab writers were convinced of a subterranean chamber under the Sphinx. He mentions that the inventory stela reads "[the God gave] the thought in his heart, of putting a written decree on the side of this [above-mentioned] Sphinx, in an hour of the night." Yet no such decree has been found. There is also the interesting fact of hieroglyphs found on the ruins of a temple east of the second Pyramid on the *inner* face of the stone, and blocks in tombs to the west of the Great Pyramid with inverted hieroglyphics on the *inward* faces.

Examination of the Sphinx shows that the inner contours of the two forepaws have been filled in with large limestone blocks which are visible where the outer double casing of brickwork is incomplete. The right hind paw can also be seen to be completely composed of such large limestone blocks. There is no record of these blocks having been examined.

East of the Sphinx, on the other side of the road leading to the Great Pyramid, is a small sand hill. One archeologist that we know of investigated this, but perhaps did not continue far enough west. He found some blackened linestone that seemed to be part of a crenellated Old Kingdom facade which he thought might have come from a small temple. Since there was supposed to have been a small pyramid over the spot where the record chamber was, this may or may not be indicative.

In some areas it is felt that the visual evidence around the Sphinx is sufficient as a basis for a thorough examination, for there is no known record of such an examination. There is almost no contemporary information on the Sphinx; who built it and why is still mainly conjecture. Foundation deposits containing such information were usually placed under most temples, so possibly some such might be found under one of the large limestone blocks composing the paws. A reference work which would comprise a complete study of the Sphinx itself is needed and would constitute a valuable contribution to Egyptology.

Scholars, historians and archeologists have for centuries added to the clues that make up the body of evidence that will perhaps one day solve a mystery which has fired the imagination throughout the ages. When the *time has been fulfilled,* the readings indicated, the clues may become keys to the mystery of Egypt.

ADVICE ON AUTOMATIC WRITING

from an Edgar Cayce Reading

Q-2. What is the source of the automatic writing I have received? Should I develop this? Please explain.

A-2. As has been given, there are the influences from without and the influences from within. Rather has the promise been, "I will be thy God and ye shall be my people. *My* Spirit shall bear witness with thy spirit, thy soul, that ye *are,* that ye *be,* the children of God." Those influences that are about thee are good, but rather *ever* let that which thou would gain through thy writing be inspired by the best in self as magnified through the Christ, than *any* ENTITY or spirit or soul! While these seek for expression ever, they be seekers as thyself. And as He gave, if the blind lead the blind *both* shall fall into the ditch. Be then led rather by that which comes from thine own soul, which thou meetest in the temple of thy body, thy God in thee. And if He uses other influences, He will direct same. Be not then *directed* save by the spirit of the Christ that is thy heritage. Faint not. Be not overcome. But use that thou has begun to develop in thyself, letting thy Master, thy God, be thy director ever. *Woe* is he that would harken to the voice that would turn thee aside. For as the prophet of old has said, if even an angel of light proclaims other than that which thy Savior has given, have none of it! In thy meditations, then, much hast thou grown in thy closeness with Him . . .

Write, yea . . . but let it be prompted by the spirit of the *Christ* with thine own spirit.   792-1

LSD AND THE CAYCE READINGS

William A. McGarey, M.D.
Director, Medical Research Division
The Edgar Cayce Foundation

Throughout a period of more than forty years, Edgar Cayce regularly lay down and went into a type of sleep from which state he could give what have come to be known as "readings." He has described the process of his going into this state as a gradual relaxation with the sudden appearance of a bright shaft of white light. Without the experience of this white light, he indicated that he could not lose consciousness to give a reading.

Meditation, as it is known in the study group program of the A.R.E., really begins in an individual's experience when there comes into the silence the appearance of the light. Paul saw a great light on the road to Damascus; cosmic consciousness has come to be a condition often associated with appearance of a light.

Recently, Milman[1] reported the story of a five-year-old girl who, while fixing breakfast for herself, found in the refrigerator, and ate, a sugar cube impregnated with LSD (lysergic acid diethylamide) belonging to her 18-year-old-uncle. Within twenty minutes she was disoriented and screaming, acutely psychotic, and was hospitalized for care. She thought her body was cut off at the waist, she maintained that her name was Dorothy, not Donna, and she passed through periods of screaming and silence. Within a period of days, most of the disturbances had disappeared. However, her thinking disorders and distortion of body image persisted. After five months, an abnormal EEG and disorganization of visual-motor functions remained. Yet LSD in others has brought the experience of light, a heightened awareness, sensations and experiences bringing to it the name of a consciousness-expanding drug.

Was the uncle who owned the LSD sugar cube searching for the same light—in this case brought about chemically—which Cayce experienced at the onset of his readings? Obviously there is need of clarification of the entire field of the psychedelic drugs as it relates to the normal physical body, the nature of the psychic experiences obtained with the use of the drugs, and the aims and purposes of the A.R.E. as an organization which is unavoidably involved in all questions dealing with the paranormal.

LSD, of course, is just one of the so-called hallucinogenics which now are many in number and which are readily obtainable in spite of federal law prohibiting their manufacture and sale. They are also called psychotomimitic, psycholytic, psychedelic, schiozphrenogenic, cataleptogenic, phantastica, mysticomimetic, and psychodysleptic; Szara[2] defines psychodysleptic as a distortion of mental functioning and on this basis selects this term as the name of choice. There is no question, however, that hallucinogenic will continue to be, with psychedelic, the name most commonly used.

Who Uses Drugs and Why?

The hallucinogenic drugs certainly are part of the world scene today, and there is as little likelihood that they will cease to exist as that we will go backward in time. Thus we must deal with the problems that they present and try to approach factually and objectively a subject which has become an emotionally turbulent portion of the lives of hundreds of thousands of people, or we will be like the ostrich that buries his head in the sand to escape notice.

Aside from accidental ingestion of an hallucinogenic drug and situations where it is being used therapeutically, most persons who use the mind-expanding medications are those of late high school or college who are well-adjusted or are borderline psychotics.[2,3,4,5,6,7] The first time a young person will take a drug it is usually an act of curiosity; the second or third time for kicks; but beyond that, the person who takes four or more doses is either isolated from life or is seriously trying to find his own balance.[3] Szara[2] states that the setting determines what will happen in the course of a "trip" with LSD. Thus, if the setting is a religious or a mystical one then this type of experience will come about. Likewise a therapeutic setting might bring about a beneficial result with hypnotic suggestion or through the means of bringing suppressions to the surface, or through a transcendental experience.

It is known that a borderline psychotic receiving the drug often reaps a very serious result. Not too well known however, is the fact that LSD may precipitate a psychotic reaction in the person with a previously good personality integration. Hensala et al.[4] saw this happen in a teacher who was hospitalized after ingestion of LSD. In their study of 20 patients admitted to a mental hospital for care for LSD ingestion, compared with 25 controls—all with psychotic symptoms—they made some very interesting observations about the nature of people who have psychotic reactions to LSD. In the control group the work history was good, while those in the LSD group worked irregularly, were petty thieves—one a male prostitute—and never held a job regularly. The sexual history in the LSD

169

group showed serious sexual psychopathology, with problems such as homosexuality, male impotence, female frigidity, promiscuity among the heterosexually oriented, and polymorphous perversions. Among the control group, on the other hand, only two of the 25 had any prior evidence of sexual disturbance. Personality characteristics revealed adolescent action patterns with antisocial behavior in the LSD group. No antisocial behavior was found in the controls. A fourth variance showed all but two in the LSD group to have had prior history of drug use, including everything from amphetamine and heroin to peyote. Out of the control group only two previously had used drugs in an unsupervised manner. These differences will be commented on later.

In trying to understand some of the drives and desires and the makeup of those individuals who are of the young college-age group, a study by Keniston[6] on the Gestalt of young college men who are alienated and distrustful, might be of significance at this point. These people search for experiences of an LSD nature. He states, "At root probably the most powerful unconscious motive in many of these young men is their desire to merge, to fuse with, to lose themselves in some embracing person, experience, or group. This fantasy of mystical fusion involves the unconscious desire to lose all self-hood in some undifferentiated state with another or with nature . . . A major component of this quest is the search for a breakthrough. The alienated value most those moments when the barriers to perception crumble, when the walls between themselves and the world fall away and they are 'in contact' with nature, other people, or themselves."

Unanswered as yet is the question imposed by those who seem to be balanced in all regards and are seeking for an expansion of consciousness through the use of drugs. These people, neither taking LSD for curiosity or kicks nor having any aspects of a borderline psychosis or any of the underlying characteristics of the psychotic as Hensala lists them, are seeking for a truly valid religious experience or an expansion of consciousness or a better understanding of themselves and the world around. It is obvious from the availability of drugs that these people may obtain their experience if they desire it enough. The question posed is his: Are they wise or foolish as it relates to their total being?

We are certainly obliged to ask at this point: What is it that draws the ostensibly normal person toward the use of the hallucinogenics? Is it his hurry to reach the point in consciousness reportedly achieved by saints and seers in ages past? Is it the desire to achieve oneness with God? With the light? Is it his desire for power of a spiritual nature which is currently not his? Is it his rebellion against Jesus' injunction in the Bible that "In your patience possess ye your souls"? (Luke 21:19)

Each person likes to consider himself normal, but each is aware that he is not perfect. A natural deduction then brings him to the understanding that he is not normal in the perfect sense—that there are areas of his physical body and awareness, of his emotions and spiritual being that are defective to one degree or another. This lays the groundwork perhaps for understanding somewhat the defective structures that lead the non-psychotic person to the use of LSD-related drugs. Those psychotic persons admitted to the mental institution after taking LSD were markedly different in their makeup from the control group who had not ingested the drug. The lack of direction and of persistence in work history speaks of emotional and consciousness makeup which are rather explicitly associated in the Cayce readings with derangement of the glandular-spiritual center known as the Cells of Leydig—also called the "water center." The sexual deviations bring attention to the same glands, which produce estrogen and testosterone, hormones which produce secondary sexual changes in the human. These, then, allow for sexual temptation and sexual deviations. The anti-social behavior is not, perhaps, as readily related as an emotion to this particular glandular area of influence, but these three differences in these psychotic patients certainly team up to make them more susceptible to using the other drugs prior to their use of the hallucinogenics.

Psychosis is not an all-or-nothing phenomenon. Rather, there are psychotic tendencies in all people, many of which, when allowed to flourish, end up in senile psychosis as the years advance. Perhaps it is the same deviation of character or personality, so well-developed in

171

the 20 cases admitted to the mental institution, which might be present to a much lesser degree in those who seek, while ostensibly normal in all regards, for the consciousness-expanding, psychedelic experience to be gained through an LSD "trip." Perhaps an abnormality in these cells, which are so obscure in the human anatomy, play a large part in such a person's impatience, his rebellion, his hurry to find the light, to break down barriers, to achieve a oneness with all things, to reach a state of spiritual superiority. All the answers are not in; of this we may be sure.

The beginning of an answer might be found in the following Cayce reading:

Q-4. *Explain what the divide between the soul and spiritual forces is? How manifest, and how we may study self to gain the approach to the divide.*

A-4. This is of the spiritual entity in its entirety. The superconscious is the divide, that oneness lying between the soul and the spirit force, within the spiritual entity. Not of earth forces at all, only awakened with the spiritual indwelling and acquired individually.

Q-5. *How may the individual think, study, and act to acquire this awakening?*

A-5. Study to show thyself approved unto Him, rightly dividing the words of truth, keeping self unspotted from the world, avoiding the appearance of evil, for as is given, those who would seek God must believe that He IS, and a rewarder of those who would seek Him.

That is, that the Creator has that oneness with the individual to make that oneness with Him. As is given in the conditions as manifest through those who would seek the oneness with God, for only those who have approached sufficient to make the mind of the soul, the mind of the spiritual, one with Him, may understand or gather that necessary to approach that understanding.   900-21

172

LSD, representative of the hallucinogenic drugs, has been called a mixed blessing, but there are volatile opinions on both sides of the fence. Until rather recently the drugs were available to be used under properly supervised conditions. However, with the restrictions put on them by the Food and Drug Administration, the work done under scientifically supervised conditions has dwindled to almost nothing. Most investigators are hesitant to use it at all because of the hue and cry that has been raised concerning the diverse effects that have been brought to light.

Kurland *et al.*[8] are among the minority that are utilizing LSD in a research setting and they report on work that has been done with the alcoholic patient. They emphasize that special training is required to use psychedelics as a therapeutic tool. Some excellent results have been forthcoming, however, in their preliminary work. Speaking of the day in which he received LSD, one patient whose case history was reported said in conclusion that "this was the most satisfying and majestic day in my life." The authors believe that LSD adds significantly to the presently available rehabilitation resources.

While the United States finds publicity mounting about the dangers of LSD, and researchers are almost fearful of utilizing it as a tool, eastern Europe[9] is accepting LSD with open arms, relatively speaking. Use is being made of the drug in treatment of alcoholism and depression. Knoblock, of the University Polyclinic in Lobec, Czechoslovakia, feels that it "breaches the divide between the therapist and the patient who withdraws from reality either through the use of alcohol or through emotion." Rather strangely, western Europe is not quite as enthusiastic as its more oriental counterpart but finds itself in between the stand taken by the United States and eastern Europe. Eng[9] has reported on 63 alcoholics treated with LSD management and 59 treated conventionally, and reports in the former fewer arrests, less delirium tremens, less absenteeism, an average of more days of total abstinence from alcohol, an average of more days of gainful employment, and no adverse nor untoward physiological or mental reactions.

In several states efforts have been made to pass laws prohibiting possession, sale, or use of these drugs. Several outstanding men have protested this effort. Walter Alvarez, M.D., in a personal letter to the Illinois legislature on February 18, 1967, pointed out that, in his opinion, "the passing of a law against LSD will serve only one purpose and that will be to interest mildly psychotic boys and girls to get some of the drug, and to try it on themselves." He pointed out that, because of the dose being so small, thousands of doses could be brought into the country in a fountain pen without detection. No purpose would be served by such a law, and it would almost put an end to legitimate research.

On the positive side of the ledger also are reports of its use in terminal cancer patients. Results from this study have not been fully reported and are not available for evaluation here.

It is not within the scope of this paper to comment extensively and exhaustively on the subject of the hallucinogenics, but it would be rather an avoidance of fact if a few of the many books on the psychedelic drugs were not mentioned. Newland,[10] Clark,[11] Puharich,[12] and Weil et al.,[13] are four who have published books discussing the effects on the consciousness of the hallucinogenic drugs. None of these report all the attendant dangers.

Downing[3] states that both LSD and marijuana are safe physiologically—that is, they have no adverse effects on the total physiological functioning of the human body. This is an illusion which many who advocate the promiscuous use of the hallucinogenics would have accepted as truth. More and more evidence keeps coming to light which points out that LSD, like other potent drugs, can be markedly detrimental to the body, and this of course applies to the physiological processes of the body. One does not yet know what the final effect will be on the 5-year-old girl whose case has already been discussed. Egozcue[14,15] reports on cell abnormalities which are linked to the ingestion of LSD. Chromosomal breaks, they have found, occur two to three times as frequently in children of women who have used high doses of LSD during pregnancy, as in the normal child. These breaks, of course, appear also in the mother and have been found in genetic studies in most cases of individuals who have been taking LSD. One child whose mother had taken 1000 mcg, of LSD during pregnancy had a leukocyte chromosome resembling the Philadelphia chromosome, which has been associated with chronic myologenous leukemia, and has not been seen in normal cultures.

Egozcue points out that in his studies, the abnormal chromosomal breaks do not occur when a person has taken less than 300 mcg. doses—even if many doses are taken. Thus, apparently, a dose of 300 mcg. is critical in the study that he has performed to date, which involves 70 patients. The implication of such genetic changes, certainly, cannot be overemphasized and certainly points to the fact that LSD, in an unsupervised situation, is not safe. Other physiological effects, much less dramatic and far-reaching in their implications, but just as potent when considering areas of consciousness, come about on nearly any dosage level. The changes have not been assessed in the nervous system function nor in the cells of this vital area. But the mind, the nervous system, consciousness as a total thing, are associated with the dramatic transformations in awareness, in mind-capacity, brought about by these drugs. In the absence of a solid personality makeup, it is not surprising that individuals have lost their lives through unsuccessful attempts to fly—without aid of wings—or have been killed while walking down a freeway, thinking themselves to be invisible.

Untoward results of LSD ingestion such as these, associated with prolonged adverse reactions, and recurrent episodes which may come about as long as a year after the initial taking of the drug, as well as adverse reactions on carefully screened patients while in a supervised setting lead several investigators[16],[17],[18] to conclude that it cannot be predicted at the present time who will have a bad experience, even in the hands of qualified supervisors, and that it is potentially dangerous in all circumstances. A final judgment, they say, regarding the potential uses of LSD must be held in abeyance.

LSD and the Pineal

The pineal gland has been associated with the third eye in metaphysical literature almost as far back as such references exist. It is rather uniquely related to physical existing conditions in that one type of lizard has an actual third eye situated under the epidermis which is part of the pineal gland in that organism and which has all the capabilities of sight. In the human being, cone cells of the pineal gland have been found to be identical microscopically with cone cells found in the macula of the retina of the eye. The macula is the only portion of the retina which perceives color. The pineal cone cells, in addition to producing hormones, are directly connected to nerves of the autonomic nervous system arising from the superior cervical ganglion of the sympathetic chain. Thus the pineal parallels the eye in many regards. It is associated with the inner, autonomic nervous system rather than the cerebral structures which are associated with outer, conscious activities. Much in the same manner, psychic revelations, visions, and LSD experiences are perceived inwardly while the eye sees the outer world.

Work which is being pursued in Chile and reported recently by Naranjo[19] leads us to a rather fascinating concept which may give a clue to the real mode of action of the psychedelic drugs. He reported on the first endogenous hallucinogen, 6-methoxytetrahydroharman which is formed in vivo from 5-methoxytryptamine and acetaldehyde and is chemically identical with the pineal gland hormone in animals which is called adrenoglomerulotropine. He implicates the pineal in still another hallucinogenic substance, 6-methoxyharmalan formed in vitro from melatonin, which is obtained from the methylation of acetyl-serotonin, a reaction made possible by an enzyme present only in the pineal gland. This enzyme is hydroxyindole O-methyl transferase (HIOMT).

Naranjo's work, while it does not prove relationships, certainly points toward the pineal as the originator of the production within the body of what is called an hallucinogenic substance. Thus, any creative activity within the body which results in a particular activity of the pineal gland could bring about a type of transcendental experience.

While many questions concerning the mechanism of such a reaction remain unanswered, this would still give one a rather interesting explanation of what is involved in the occurrence of the visions of mystics, the vivid imagery in dreams, the light which Cayce saw at the beginning of his readings, and the cosmic consciousness type of reaction which has become almost common knowledge in this day and age. It points up rather vividly the difference between these experiences and the experiences of a drug-induced state using any of the hallucinogenics. One originates from within the human body as the natural process of a growth or a change which allows the pineal to become activated to such an extent that it might originate the production of endogenous hallucinogens. The drug-induced hallucinogenic state, on the other hand, superimposes a condition on the body that is not natural and for which it perhaps is not prepared nor capable of handling.

Further developments in this particular field should be extremely interesting to follow. It is Naranjo's opinion that harmalan, which is obtained from the seeds of *Peganum harmala*, and which is related to those 6-methoxy hormones already discussed, produce in the human being a purer hallucinogenic effect than LSD and other related hallucinogens.

Edgar Cayce, the A.R.E. and LSD

In my opinion, throughout the readings Edgar Cayce seemed to be talking about this question of LSD along with many other questions that we face in daily life. He saw the world in action, and us as a part of that action. Thus, he would see a question as being properly answered through acting in accordance with certain principles which were always the same. He saw healing in the physical body as coming about through patience, persistence, and consistency. All problems were to be met in the same manner, by the application of these principles of truth which he said had existed from the beginning of creation—understanding, patience, kindness, forgiveness, these things called the fruits of the spirit.

Cayce urged, time and again, that the fast way is never the best, since lasting results must be built line upon line, precept upon precept, here a little, there a little. Everything, he said, must be done in decency and order. Any activity or decision contrary to these principles was an act of rebellion, simply because it was not in cooperation with and in obedience to the principles. Rebellion, he said, was part of our nature that leads us away from the creative energy that we call God:

[We were] in the beginning, celestial beings. We have first the Son, then the other sons or celestial beings that are given their force and power.

Hence that force which rebelled in the unseen forces (or in spirit), that came into activity, was that influence which has been called Satan, the Devil, the Serpent; they are One. That of rebellion! Hence, when man in any activity rebels against the influences of good he harkens to the influence of evil rather than the influence of good.

Hence, will is given to man as he comes into the manifested form that we see in material forces, for the choice. As given, "there is set before thee (man) good and evil."

Evil is rebellion. Good is the Son of Life, of Light, of Truth; and the Son of Light, of Life, of Truth came into physical being to demonstrate and show and lead the way for man's ascent to the power of good over evil in the material world.

As there is, then, a personal savior, there is the personal devil.   262-52

It appears to me that Cayce here was speaking about those who would take LSD for spiritual enlightenment. He said time after time that there was one way, and that was the way of the Christ. If we are to climb up another way we become thieves and robbers to ourselves. It would seem rather clear that in this he was saying that we should use meditation as a means of total growth of the being.

The following two statements seem to pursue the same course:

So, know ye the way; point it out. For, as He has given, though ye come to the altar or to thine church or to thine neighbor pleading not for self but for others, and it is that ye may be exalted, that ye may be honored, that ye may be spoken well of, for others; He cannot hear thy petition. Why? Because

178

there has another entered with thee into thy chamber, thy closet, and He, thy God—that answers prayer, that forgives through his Son . . . is shut out. In His name then only; for, as He gave, "they that climb up some other way are thieves and robbers."   262-77

A.1 . . . He, though He were the Son, earned obedience through the things which He suffered. He that climbs up any other way than accepting those things that are to be met day by day, even as He, seeks through some other channel. The servant may never be greater than the master. He has given that we may be equal and one with Him, yet through Him, His manifestations, in Him, we live in the earth, we move and have our being.   262-46

Interspersed throughout nearly all these 14,238 readings, we sense the urgency in Cayce's repetitive advice to choose a spiritual ideal and then always to act in accordance with the ideal that has been chosen. He urges us to use the wisdom that has been given us over the ages as a guide, to consider the body a holy thing, a temple of God. We are advised to be patient—not to be in a hurry—to be unselfish and not to seek to build the self image and the ego in the areas that cry for gratification.

It is difficult to imply any advice from the readings other than that LSD, as a drug for spiritual enlightenment, should be avoided and has inherent within it dangers which make it harmful to those who use it.

When considering the advisability of using the hallucinogenics in a therapeutic setting, it is again questionable whether Edgar Cayce would have suggested it had it been available while he was alive. For in all the physical readings, his therapies seemed to be aimed at improving the function of a cell, an organ, or a system of activities within the body. It was rare that he would suggest anything which did not assist in meeting the needs of the condition present. The hallucinogenic drugs impose upon the body an artificial condition that is not consistent with the development of functional capacity of the pineal gland. Thus they do not influence function but rather precipitate changes which are likely to bring about a more unbalanced physiology than was present in the beginning. Yet, there have been alcoholics and depressive psychotics who have undoubtedly been influenced for the better by the use of LSD. Cayce suggested the use of surgery or strong medicine on occasion. He apparently intended to correct the condition present, in order that the individual might be better able after physical healing, to grow in consciousness. He saw healing as many things, but from one source.

Thus, I suspect that where the hallucinogenic drugs have been used in selected cases as a promising therapeutic tool, Cayce might have approved. The following would apparently imply this:

> For all healing comes from the One source. And, whether there is the application of foods, exercise, medicine, or even the knife,—it is to bring [to] the conciousness of the Forces within the body, that aid in reproducing themselves which is the awareness of Creative or God Forces. 2692-1

Summary

It is my feeling that Cayce, in his work of a lifetime, must certainly be interpreted as saying that we should view the hallucinogenic drugs with a great deal of caution, that they become dangerous to our total growth under most circumstances.

From the medical literature, summaries that have a degree of caution in regard to the use of LSD under any circumstances are common. Farnsworth[20] is perhaps most dramatic and to the point in his opinion that "in short, our professional medical opinion is that playing with LSD is a desperately dangerous form of 'drug roulette.' The medical evidence is clear. Any person taking LSD runs the clear risk of psychotic breakdown and long-run physiological damage."

We have the hallucinogenics with us. We must choose for ourselves always, and for others frequently. It is of vital importance that we look clearly at our choice of directions, and all of the implications that are involved in a path which, in the final analysis, is a spiritual one

180

through a material earth. The unconscious information through Cayce and the conscious information through the science of medicine come together rather vividly in showing us a direction.

References

1. Milman, D.H.: "An Untoward Reaction to Accidental Ingestion of LSD in a 5-Year-Old Girl," *JAMA* 201: 143-147 (Sept. 11, 1967).

2. Szara, S.: "The Hallucinogenic Drugs—Curse or Blessing?" *Amer J Psychiat* 123: 1513-1517 (June 1967).

3. Downing, J.: "Something's Happening," *Medical Opinion & Review* 3:100-108 (Sept 1967).

4. Hensala, J.D.; Epstein, L.J.; and Blacker, K.H.: "LSD and Psychiatric Inpatients," *Arch Gen Psychiat* 16:554-559 (May 1967).

5. Bowers, M., *et al.*: "Dynamics of Psychedelic Drug Abuse," *Arch Gen Psychiat* 16: 560-566 (May 1967).

6. Keniston, K.; as quoted by Bowers, M. *et al.*: "Dynamics of Psychedelic Drug Abuse," *Arch Gen Psychiat* 16:563 (May 1967).

7. Alexander, E.J.: "LSD—An Outsider's Viewpoint," *Henry Ford Hosp Med Bull* 15:23-26 (March 1967).

8. Kurland, A.A., *et al.*: "Psychedelic Therapy Utilizing LSD in the Treatment of the Alcoholic Patient: A Preliminary Report," *Amer J Psychiat* 123:1203-1209 (April 1967).

9. "Europeans Find LSD 'Trip' Can be Therapeutic," *Medical World News* 8:50 (June 16, 1967).

10. Newland, C.A.: *My Self and I* (New York: New American Library of World Literature, Inc., 1963).

11. Clark, F.M.: *Beyond the Light* (New York: Vantage Press Inc., 1958).

12. Puharich, A.: *The Sacred Mushroom* (New York: Doubleday and Co., Inc., 1959).

13. Weil, G.; Metzner, R.; and Leary, T., eds: *The Psychedelic Reader* (New York: University Books, Inc., 1965).

14. "Cell Abnormalities Linked to LSD," Medical News, *JAMA* 200 (May 29, 1967) adv. p. 29, 30.

15. "Chromosome Breaks in LSD Users' Infants," *Medical Tribune* 8:1, 21 (Sept. 21, 1967).

16. Kleber, H.D.: "Prolonged Adverse Reactions from Unsupervised Use of Hallucinogenic Drugs," *J Nerv Ment Dis* 144:308-319 (April 1967).

17. Ungerleider, J.T., and Fisher, D.D.: "The Problems of LSD[25] and Emotional Disorders," *Cal Med* 106:49 (Jan. 1967).

18. Robbins, M.D.; Frosch, W.A.; and Stern, M.: "Further Observations on Untoward Reactions to LSD," *Amer J Pychiat* 124:393-395 (Sept. 1967.)

19. "Chilean Study Yields Hallucinogen That May Give Clues to Psychosis," *Medical Tribune* 8 (Feb. 22, 1967) 2.

20. Farnsworth, D.L., and Prout, C.: "Marijuana and LSD," The Bulletin, San Francisco Medical Society 40 (June, 1967), 16, 17.

THE MEANING OF WISDOM

from the Edgar Cayce Readings

Yes, we have the group as gathered here; as a group, as individuals, and their work under the lesson Wisdom.

In continuing with the discussion upon the Wisdom of the Father, let first each of you attune yourselves to that consciousness as may be had through attuning self in this meditation:

"OUR FATHER, WHO ART IN THE HEAVEN OF OUR OWN CONSCIOUSNESS, SO ATTUNE MY MIND, MY BODY, WITH THE INFINITE LOVE THOU HAST SHOWN TO THE CHILDREN OF MEN, THAT I IN BODY, IN MIND, MAY KNOW THE WISDOM OF THE FATHER IN JESUS, THE CHRIST."

Then, it behooves each to be more aware of that love as brings into the experience of each soul the understanding that we as individuals cannot bear the cross of life alone but that the Father in His Wisdom has given to each an ensample, a promise to the children of man . . . "which is indeed mine now if I will but choose the love of Jesus in my daily life, in my walks among my fellow man."

In Wisdom thou wilt not find fault. In Wisdom thou wilt not condemn any. In Wisdom thou wilt not cherish grudges. In Wisdom thou wilt love those, even those that despitefully use thee; even those that speak unkindly.

"In the Wisdom of Jesus do I claim the promises of God and know His Presence. Though in those things that are not always understood it is His

183

Wisdom that makes for the changing of the affairs of the material experiences, the environs, the opportunities for those who profess their faith to give of themselves in body, in mind, that they may indeed know the Wisdom of God in their experiences."

KNOW THAT THE Wisdom of Jesus . . . that is the promise to all . . . is a part of the daily life, and not be to put on as a coat or a cloak, but to be part and parcel of each and every entity.

This is the Wisdom to know, "As I purpose in my heart to do, it is in accord with that I profess with my mouth." It is Wisdom that the acts of the body, of the mind, be in accordance with that proclaimed to thy children, to thy neighbor, to thy friend, to thy foe.

For Life is in its material activity the Wisdom of the Father that men may everywhere manifest, that they . . . too . . . may be a part of the consciousness of the Cosmic Consciousness.

For as the ways of life become more complex, individuals are rather the material than the mental and spiritual.

Yet to thee, to whom the Book of Life . . . yes, the record of thine experience . . . has been opened, there is the awareness that ye are indeed the children of God. And as children in thy Wisdom ye may approach boldly the Throne of Mercy. For the prayers of the righteous are heard, for they have attuned in Wisdom to the God-Consciousness within, and have come to the realization that they are not alone but that He walketh and He talketh with those who have called upon His Name, and who day by day show forth in their conversation their love. For Jesus is the Way, Jesus is the Christ, Jesus is the Mediator, Jesus is Wisdom to those who will harken to do His biddings.

And as He hath given, "If ye love me, keep my commandments; for they are not grievous to bear. For I will bear them with thee; I will wipe away thy tears; I will comfort the brokenhearted; I will bring aid to those in the ways that are in the Wisdom of

God for thy expressions through each experience, in each activity of thine."

For thy soul in its Wisdom seeketh expression with Him. Smother it not in the doubts and the fears of materiality but in the spirit of love and truth that encompasseth all, and that is open to ye who have set thy hearts, thy faces, toward the love that is to Jesus, thy Friend, thy Brother.

These, my brethren . . . yea, these my beloved children . . . Know that in Him is the truth, the light. Ye have seen a great light. Ye have touched upon the Wisdom of the Father, as is shown in the Son.

Then make thy paths straight. Let thy conversation, thy wishes, thy desires be rather as one with Him who thought it not robbery to be equal with God.

Ye know the way. Do ye stumble in ignorance or in selfishness? Do ye doubt for the gratifying of thy body or for the fulfilling of the body-appetites?

Ye know the way. Let, then, that love of the Infinite fire thee to action, to doing! and indeed live as hath been shown.

Study to show thyself in body, in mind, approved unto that thou hast chosen in the words of Jesus the Master, thy Brother . . . in dividing the words of life in such measures that all who know thee, yes that contact thee, take cognizance of the fact that thou walkest and thou talkest with Jesus day by day; keeping thyself in body, in mind, unspotted from the world.

This is the Wisdom of God and is thine if ye will but claim it as thine own.

And may the grace and the mercy and the peace of a life lived in thine own consciousness be thine through Him that is able to present our lives before the throne of God spotless, white as snow, washed in the blood of the sacrificing made in our own daily experience . . . even as He has shown us the way. We are through.   262-105

THE A.R.E. TODAY

Out of the wealth of material in the Cayce files grew the Association for Research and Enlightenment, Inc., and its affiliated organizations, the A.R.E. Press and the Edgar Cayce Foundation.

The Foundation is engaged in the complicated task of indexing and cross-indexing the hundreds of subjects discussed in the readings. Because of their age, the papers are rapidly deteriorating, and they are now being microfilmed for safekeeping and duplicated for ready reference. The subject matter almost blankets the field of human thought; from the value of peanuts to the building of the Great Pyramid; from how to get rid of pinworms to prophecy of the future.

The Association for Research and Enlightenment is an open-membership, nonprofit organization chartered under the laws of the Commonwealth of Virginia to carry on psychic research. It is devoted to the study of the readings and conducts numerous experiments in psychic phenomena. It also cooperates in the fields of medicine, psychology and theology. The active membership of the A.R.E., as it is usually called, is made up of people of all religious faiths and many nationalities, including foreign countries. Strangely, they all seem to be able to reconcile their faiths with the philosophy emerging from the Cayce readings. They come from all walks of life; there are doctors, lawyers, ministers, artists, businessmen, teachers, students, working people, housewives.

The Association, governed by a board of trustees, conducts conferences at the Virginia Beach headquarters and regional conferences in New York, Dallas, Denver, Los Angeles and other large cities.

The Association and its affiliated organizations occupy a large, rambling, three-story frame building of shore architecture. Standing on the highest elevation at Virginia Beach, the building and grounds take up a full city block and face the Atlantic Ocean, a block away. A new building has been constructed which houses a lecture hall, class rooms, offices and the A.R.E. Press.

Hundreds of visitors come every year. With the steadily growing membership and interest, a growing staff handles volumes of inquiries, special requests, lecture announcements and literature. Visitors are shown about the plant and grounds with its broad, tiled veranda overlooking the ocean. The library containing indexed copies of 90% of the readings is of special interest.

To the skeptic there is an appropriate answer: in the words of Abraham Lincoln, "No man has a good enough memory to be a successful liar!" for forty-three years.

EDGAR CAYCE ON DREAMS
by Harmon Hartzell Bro, Ph.D.
(54-776, 75¢)

Edgar Cayce shows you how to use your dreams to achieve the same self-understanding, happiness and success he gave to others in his famous "Life Readings." By following Cayce's techniques of dream interpretations, you will be able to:
* predict the future
* discover hidden personal talents
* relieve nervous tensions
* make money
* rear children wisely
* develop your ESP
* discover your past lives
* gain insight into your destiny in this life—and beyond

HOW TO TELL FORTUNES WITH CARDS
by Wenzell Brown

This modern guide to one of the most mysterious and ancient occult sciences shows you how to tell your own fortune—and the fortunes of friends! All you need is a deck of playing cards to foresee the future!
(52-646, 50¢)

MODERN NUMEROLOGY
by Morris C. Goodman

The occult symbolism of numbers is revealed to you in this easy-to-follow guide. Discover and understand your inner self, change the course of your future—without any previous knowledge of numerology!
(53-734, 60¢)

If you are unable to obtain these books from your local dealer, they may be ordered directly from the publisher.

PAPERBACK LIBRARY
Department B
315 Park Avenue South
New York, N.Y. 10010

Please send me the books I have checked.
I am enclosing payment plus 10¢ per copy to cover postage and handling.

Name ....

Address ....

City .... State ....:.. Zip Code ....

————— Please send me your free mail order catalog